The

Jewish Americans

Consulting Editors

Ann Orlov
Managing Editor, Harvard
Encyclopedia of American
Ethnic Groups

M. Mark Stolarik
*President, The Balch Institute
for Ethnic Studies, Philadelphia*

Daniel Patrick Moynihan
*U.S. Senator from New York,
Senior Consulting Editor*

THE IMMIGRANT EXPERIENCE

The

Jewish Americans

Howard Muggamin

Sandra Stotsky, General Editor
Harvard University Graduate School of Education

CHELSEA HOUSE PUBLISHERS

New York • Philadelphia

CHELSEA HOUSE PUBLISHERS

Editorial Director: Richard Rennert
Executive Managing Editor: Karyn Gullen Browne
Copy Chief: Robin James
Picture Editor: Adrian G. Allen
Creative Director: Robert Mitchell
Art Director: Joan Ferrigno
Production Manager: Sallye Scott

THE IMMIGRANT EXPERIENCE

Editors: Rebecca Stefoff and Reed Ueda

Staff for THE JEWISH AMERICANS

Assistant Editor: Annie McDonnell
Copy Editor: Apple Kover
Assistant Designer: Stephen Schildbach
Cover Illustrator: Jane Sterrett

3 5 7 9 8 6 4

Library of Congress Cataloging-in-Publication Data

Muggamin, Howard.
    The Jewish Americans / Howard Muggamin. — [Rev. ed.]
    p. cm.—(The immigrant experience)
    Includes bibliographical references and index.
    Summary: Discusses the history, culture, and religion of the Jews, factors encouraging their emigration, and their acceptance as an ethnic group in North America.
    ISBN 0-7910-3365-1.
        0-7910-3387-2 (pbk.)
    1. Jews—United States—Juvenile literature. 2. United States—Ethnic relations—Juvenile literature. [I. Jews—United States—History. 2. Ethnic relations.] I. Title. II. Series.
E184.J5M84   1995   95-19690
973′.04924—dc20   CIP
                                                                                          AC

CONTENTS

Introduction: "A Nation of Nations"   7

Jews in America   13

Who Are the Jews?   19

Waves of Immigration   37

Life in America   51

Picture Essay: A New York Montage   65

Jewish Culture, American Culture   79

Education and Advancement   101

Jewish Americans Today   117

Further Reading   123

Index   124

THE IMMIGRANT EXPERIENCE

A LAND OF IMMIGRANTS

THE AFRICAN AMERICANS

THE AMERICAN INDIANS

THE AMISH

THE ARAB AMERICANS

THE CHINESE AMERICANS

THE CUBAN AMERICANS

THE GERMAN AMERICANS

THE GREEK AMERICANS

THE HAITIAN AMERICANS

ILLEGAL ALIENS

THE IRISH AMERICANS

THE ITALIAN AMERICANS

THE JAPANESE AMERICANS

THE JEWISH AMERICANS

THE KOREAN AMERICANS

THE LEBANESE CHRISTIANS

THE MEXICAN AMERICANS

THE POLISH AMERICANS

THE PUERTO RICANS

THE RUSSIAN AMERICANS

Other titles in preparation

CHELSEA HOUSE PUBLISHERS

A
NATION OF
NATIONS

Daniel Patrick Moynihan

The Constitution of the United States begins: "We the People of the United States. . ." Yet, as we know, the United States was not then and is not now made up of a single group of people. It is made up of many peoples. Immigrants and bondsmen from Europe, Asia, Africa, and Central and South America came here or were brought here, and still they come. They forged one nation and made it their own. More than 100 years ago, Walt Whitman expressed this great central fact of America: "Here is not merely a nation, but a teeming Nation of nations."

Although the ingenuity and acts of courage of these immigrants, our ancestors, shaped the North American way of life, we sometimes take their contributions for granted. This fine series, *The Immigrant Experience*, examines the experiences and contributions of different immigrant groups and how these contributions determined the future of the United States and Canada.

Immigrants did not abandon their ethnic traditions when they reached the shores of North America. Each ethnic group had its own customs and traditions, and each brought different experiences, accomplishments, skills, values, styles of dress, and tastes in food that lingered long after its arrival. Yet this profusion of differences created a singularity, or bond, among the immigrants.

The United States and Canada are unusual in this respect. Whereas religious and ethnic differences have sparked intolerance throughout the rest of the world—from the 17th-century religious wars to the 19th-century nationalist movements in Europe to the near extermination of the Jewish people under Nazi Germany—North Americans have struggled to learn how to respect each other's differences and live in harmony.

Our two countries are hardly the only two in which different groups must learn to live together. There is no nation of significant size anywhere in the world which would not be classified as multi-ethnic. But only in North America are there so *many* different groups, most of them living cheek by jowl with one another.

This is not easy. Look around the world. And it has not always been easy for us. Witness the exclusion of Chinese immigrants, and for practical purposes Japanese also, in the late 19th century. But by the late 20th century, Chinese and Japanese Americans were the most successful of all the groups recorded by the census. We have had prejudice aplenty, but it has been resisted and recurrently overcome.

The remarkable ability of Americans to live together as one people was seriously threatened by the issue of slavery. Thousands of settlers from the British Isles had arrived in the colonies as indentured servants, agreeing to work for a specified number of years on farms or as apprentices in return for passage to America and room and board. When the first Africans arrived in the then-British colonies during the 17th century, some colonists thought that they too should be treated as indentured servants. Eventually, the question of whether the Africans should be treated as indentured, like the English, or as slaves who could be owned for life was considered in a Maryland court. The court's calamitous decree held that blacks were slaves bound to a lifelong servitude, and so also were their children. America went through a time of moral examination and civil war before it finally freed African slaves and their descendants. The principle that all people are created equal had faced its greatest challenge and survived.

Yet the court ruling that set blacks apart from other races fanned flames of discrimination that burned long after slavery was abolished—and that still flicker today. Indeed, it was about the time of the American Civil War that European theories of evolution were turned to the service of ranking different peoples by their presumed distance from our apelike ancestors.

When the Irish flooded American cities to escape the famine in Ireland, the cartoonists caricatured the typical "Paddy" (a common term for Irish immigrants) as an apelike creature with jutting jaw and sloping forehead.

By the 20th century, racism and ethnic prejudice had given rise to virulent theories of a Northern European master race. When Adolf Hitler came to power in Germany in 1933, he popularized the notion of an Aryan race. Only a man of the deepest ignorance and evil could have done this. *Aryan* is a Sanskrit word, which is to say the ancient script of what we now think of as India. It means "noble" and was adopted by linguists—notably by a fine German scholar, Max Müller—to denote the Indo-European family of languages. Müller was horrified that anyone could think of it in terms of race, especially a race of blond-haired, blue-eyed Teutons. But the Nazis embraced the notion of a master race. Anyone with darker and heavier features was considered inferior. Buttressed by these theories, the German Nazi state from 1933 to 1945 set out to destroy European Jews, along with Poles, Gypsies, Russians, and other groups considered inferior. It nearly succeeded. Millions of these people were murdered.

The tragedies brought on by ethnic and racial intolerance throughout the world demonstrate the importance of North America's efforts to create a society free of prejudice and inequality.

A relatively recent example of the New World's desire to resolve ethnic friction nonviolently is the solution that the Canadians found to a conflict between two ethnic groups. A long-standing dispute as to whether Canadian culture was properly English or French resurfaced in the mid-1960s, dividing the peoples of the French-speaking Province of Quebec from those of the English-speaking provinces. Relations grew tense, then bitter, then violent. The Royal Commission on Bilingualism and Biculturalism was established to study the growing crisis and to propose measures to ease the tensions. As a result of the commission's recommendations, all official documents and statements from the national government's capital at Ottawa are now issued in both French and English, and bilingual education is encouraged.

The year 1980 marked a coming of age for the United States's ethnic heritage. For the first time, the U.S. Bureau of the Census asked people about their ethnic background. Americans chose from more than 100 groups, including French Basque, Spanish Basque, French Canadian, African-American, Peruvian, Armenian, Chinese, and Japanese. The ethnic group with the largest response was English (49.6 million). More than 100 million Americans claimed ancestors from the British Isles, which includes England, Ireland, Wales, and Scotland. There were almost as many Germans (49.2 million) as English. The Irish-American population (40.2 million) was third, but the next-largest ethnic group, the African-Americans, was a distant fourth (21 million). There was a sizable group of French ancestry (13 million) as well as of Italian (12 million). Poles, Dutch, Swedes, Norwegians, and Russians followed. These groups, and other smaller ones, represent the wondrous profusion of ethnic influences in North America.

Canada too has learned more about the diversity of its population. Studies conducted during the French/English conflict showed that Canadians were descended from Ukrainians, Germans, Italians, Chinese, Japanese, native Indians, and Inuit, among others. Canada found it had no ethnic majority, although nearly half of its immigrant population had come from the British Isles. Canada, like the United States, is a land of immigrants for whom mutual tolerance is a matter of reason as well as principle. But note how difficult this can be in practice, even for persons of manifest goodwill.

The people of North America are the descendants of one of the greatest migrations in history. And that migration is not over.

Koreans, Vietnamese, Nicaraguans, Cubans, and many others are heading for the shores of North America in large numbers. This mix of cultures shapes every aspect of our lives. To understand ourselves, we must know something about our diverse ethnic ancestry. Nothing so defines the North American nations as the motto on the Great Seal of the United States: *E Pluribus Unum*—Out of Many, One.

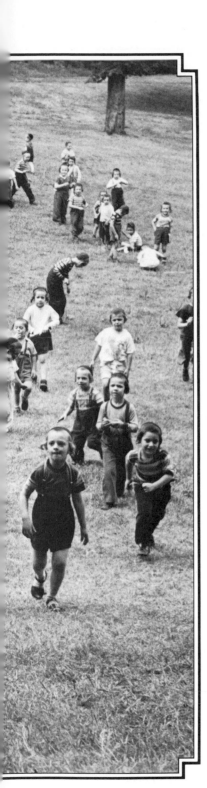

Orthodox Jewish boys play during a group outing.

JEWS IN AMERICA

Few ethnic groups or religious minorities have reached this country's shores with a history as long and troubled as that of the Jews. Those who arrived here in the 19th and early 20th centuries could look back on nearly 3,000 years of persecution: They had been enslaved in ancient Egypt in approximately 1000 B.C. and banished from their Palestinian homeland in A.D. 135. Once in exile, Jews scattered across Europe and the Middle East, searching in vain for a country that would welcome them. They found at best fleeting periods of tolerance, often followed by a backlash of anti-Semitic violence.

Although some Jews had immigrated to America as early as the 17th century, the first significant wave of Jewish immigration occurred from 1830–60, when approximately 144,000 German Jews came to seek their fortunes in the United States. Many of these newcomers established small businesses, and some transformed their initial holdings into retail empires. Within a generation, German Jews had become a prosperous group that had won the respect and acceptance of their non-Jewish compatriots.

By the end of the century, however, these respected citizens felt their great success threatened—not by events occurring in America but by developments taking place in Europe. In the 1880s a wave of anti-Semitic violence swept through Russia and eastern Poland—the countries containing the largest Jewish populations in Europe. Droves of persecuted Jews fled to America, not simply to better their economic prospects, as their German predecessors had, but to save their lives.

Between the 1880s and the 1920s, steamships brought 3.5 million eastern European Jews into New York Harbor, many of them arriving with empty pockets. Before long, this mass of immigrants had risen to become one of the most accomplished ethnic communities in America. Jewish Americans have sat on the Supreme Court, held distinguished professorships at the nation's best universities, and won every conceivable award in literature, the arts, and the sciences (including numerous Nobel Prizes). Jewish Americans have shaped the tastes of their neighbors through Hollywood films, in dramas and musicals that have dominated the Broadway stage, and in concert halls throughout America. They also had a mighty influence on the growth of investment banking and finance—hence, on the vitality of the economy.

There has been much speculation about the reasons for the remarkable success of the Jewish Americans. One factor in their success has surely been education. The Jews have a long history of respect for learning; the impoverished Jews of eastern Europe looked up to the scholars among them who devoted their lives to studying the Bible and the Talmud, a written code of Jewish law. In western Europe, the Jewish tradition of intellectual rigor produced many erudite, creative individuals.

The majority of Jewish Americans are descendants of poor, uneducated refugees from eastern Europe who had no opportunity to excel outside the narrow confines of the *shtetls,* or provincial Old World villages, where they lived. But once immigrants from these deprived places reached America, they and their children were able to satisfy their thirst for knowledge. The result was an extraordinarily well-educated ethnic community.

Today some 80 percent of America's Jews have been to college, and half of those hold advanced degrees. The ranks of American Jews have produced a large number of accomplished scholars and scientists, including Nobel Prize–winning physicist Rosalyn Yalow, literary critic Lionel Trilling, and Jonas Salk and Albert Sabin, discoverers of the polio vaccine.

American Jews have similarly been driven by the desire to better their economic and social status. The eastern European Jews who immigrated to this country between 1881 and 1924 quickly reaped material rewards. The percentage of workers holding white-collar jobs (as opposed to blue-collar, or manual, jobs) easily surpasses the rate among the general population. And Jews account for a large number of the nation's physicians, lawyers, and professors.

Though the first generation of immigrant Jews prospered mainly by running small businesses, today Jewish Americans can be found in the boardrooms of the nation's most powerful corporations. This change was dramatized in 1973 when a Jewish executive, Irving S. Shapiro, assumed the position of chairman and chief executive officer at E. I. du Pont de Nemours and Company, one of the country's oldest and most prestigious companies.

New York's Educational Alliance library served immigrants eager to learn about life in America.

The United States is home to 7 million Jews, out of a world population of slightly more than 14 million. (Another 3.5 million Jews live in Israel, 2 million in the countries of the former Soviet Union, 1 million in western Europe, mostly in Britain and France, and 300,000 in Canada.) Traditionally, the majority of Jews in the United States have lived in the northeastern states, heavily clustered in and around New York City, but that is changing: in 1990, only 40 percent of American Jews lived in the Northeast, although well over half of these northeastern Jews were concentrated in the New York area. Jews are moving into the midwestern and southern states, but the largest concentrations of American Jewish population outside New York are in California and Florida. In 1990, Los Angeles had a Jewish population of more than half a million, and more than 300,000 Jews lived in Miami, Florida.

Jews account for only about 2.75 percent of the total U.S. population. The birthrate among American Jews is lower than that of the population at large; in 1990 the

A bride and groom take their vows beneath the khupe, *a traditional Jewish wedding canopy.*

average Jewish family had 1.7 children, compared with 2.1 for the national average. This lower birthrate, combined with the fact that Jewish Americans today are as likely to marry non-Jews as to marry Jews, means that the Jewish American population is slowly shrinking as a percentage of the total national population. For decades observers have predicted that intermarriage and assimilation would bring an end to Jewish culture in America, but so far this has not happened. American Jews have retained a high degree of Jewish consciousness while remaining deeply committed Americans.

Religious Jews generally fall into three groupings: Orthodox, Conservative, and Reform. Orthodox Jews, the most traditional, interpret the biblical Old Testament as the word of God and attempt to obey its strictures to the letter. Conservative Jews regard their religion as a dynamic one and feel that the Old Testament must be continually reinterpreted to meet the needs of changing times. Reform Judaism, which has been shaped to a large extent by American Jews, views the faith as a form of ethical monotheism (belief in a single god) whose meaning may differ for each believer. Reform Jews reject some of the ancient traditions—such as dietary laws and services conducted entirely in the Hebrew language—that are followed by Orthodox and Conservative Jews. In addition to reflecting a broad spectrum of religious views, American Jews are ethnically diverse. Although a great many of the early Jewish immigrants came from Germany or eastern Europe, recent years have seen an influx of Jewish immigrants from Iran, Israel, Russia, Iraq, Syria, Morocco, and other nations.

Judaism is also more than a religion; it is a culture rooted in a remarkable and often tragic history. Even Jews who never step inside a synagogue or celebrate religious holidays often consider themselves Jews and are viewed as such by their neighbors. The thorny question of Jewish identity—who, exactly, is a Jew?—will continue to be debated for years to come. ❧

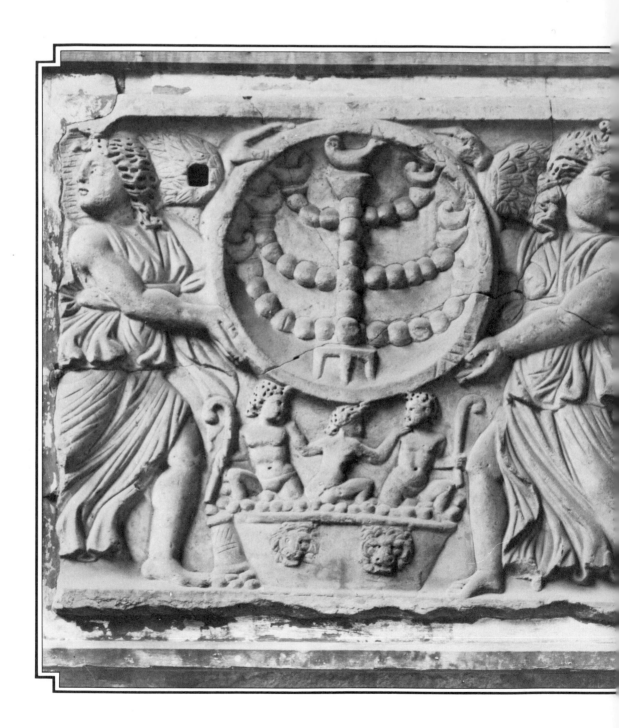

The candelabra on this carved Roman sarcophagus—from the 3rd or 4th century—identifies it as belonging to a Jew.

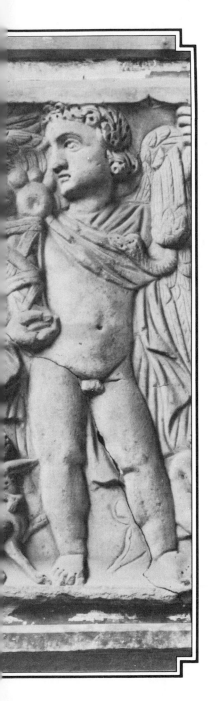

WHO ARE THE JEWS?

Are the Jews a religious or an ethnic group? According to Orthodox Jewish law a Jew is either the child of a Jewish mother or a convert to the Jewish religion. Many Jews, however, do not observe the religious dictates of Judaism, though they feel a connection to Jewish history. At the same time, Jews do not claim a unique ethnicity: They are Semites, but so are other peoples whose ancestry traces back to the Middle East and who are found from Morocco to the Persian Gulf. And Jewish populations exist in Africa, India, and the Orient.

Four thousand years ago, the ancestors of modern Jews were known as Hebrews, a tribe whose dramatic and painful story anticipates the later history of the Jewish people. In the desert surrounding the region known as Canaan, around the Jordan River, the Hebrews lived as nomads, much like other tribes of the Middle East. Three Hebrew patriarchs—Abraham, his son Isaac, and his grandson Jacob—called the land of Canaan their home. (Canaan has had many names over the centuries. Around three thousand years ago it was the site of two ancient Jewish kingdoms, Judea and Israel; in Roman times it was called Palestine; and today most of it is included in the state of Israel.)

The Dawn of Judaism

In about 1700 B.C. famine struck the Hebrews. They migrated from Canaan to Egypt, where they remained

The story of Abraham and his son Isaac was depicted by the Florentine sculptor Lorenzo Ghiberti in his Gates of Paradise, *a set of bronze doors he created between 1403 and 1424.*

until about 1280 B.C., when the pharaoh Ramses II took advantage of their vulnerable status by enslaving them. He called the refugees "strangers in a strange land," a phrase that has since come to summarize the Jews' beleaguered history. Because the laws of Egyptian society protected only property, the Hebrews could not escape servitude and saw little hope of ever regaining their freedom. Nevertheless, they recognized that as long as they remained under the pharaoh's thumb they must band together as a group to ensure their survival outside the ancient homeland.

In about 1225 B.C. there occurred the single most important event in the consolidation of Jewish identity: The prophet Moses organized the Hebrew slaves and led them out of Egypt. The biblical book Exodus describes this trek across the Red Sea into the Sinai Desert:

And Moses stretched out his hand over the sea; and the Lord caused the sea to go back by a strong east wind all that night, and made the sea dry land and the waters were divided.

And the children of Israel went into the midst of the sea upon the dry ground; and the waters were a wall unto them on their right hand, and on their left.

Their journey across the desert toward Canaan was an arduous one, but they were fortified at Mount Sinai, where Moses read the Ten Commandments from stone tablets said to have been sent down to earth by God himself. The Ten Commandments—or the Decalogue—exhorted the Jews to act in a manner governed by moral and ethical considerations: "Honor thy father and mother. . . . Thou shalt not kill. . . . Thou shalt not commit adultery. . . . Neither shalt thou bear false witness against thy neighbor. . . . " Believing that a divine voice had addressed them, the Hebrews abandoned polytheism (the worship of many spirits) and instead dedicated themselves to monotheism, the belief in a single, all-powerful deity. They called their god Yahweh, the God of the Jews. Because God had singled

Moses leads the Jews across the Red Sea in a 15th-century woodcut from a German Bible designed by Johannes Gutenberg, the father of modern printing.

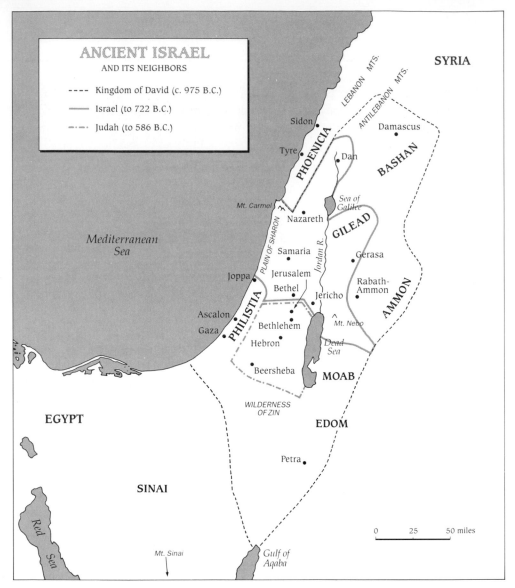

This map illustrates the boundaries of ancient Israel.

them out to be his followers, the Hebrews came to consider themselves the "chosen people."

The Kingdom of Israel

The story of these roughly 800 years—from Abraham to enslavement to freedom under the leadership of Moses—is documented in the first five books of the biblical Old Testament: Genesis, Exodus, Leviticus, Numbers, and Deuteronomy, known collectively as the Torah, the linchpin of the Jewish faith.

After leaving Mount Sinai, the ancient Jews reached the "Promised Land" of Canaan and found safe haven there, living under the benign rule of the Judges, socially progressive leaders who even admitted a woman, Deborah, to their inner circle. The Jews installed a monarchy in about 1000 B.C., and their second king, David, established Jerusalem as the capital city. But within a generation Canaan was divided into two kingdoms, Israel to the north and Judea (from which the word *Jew* originates) to the south.

This division weakened the kingdoms and perhaps contributed to the subsequent downfall of Israel in the north: In 721 B.C. this kingdom fell first to the Assyrians and later to the Babylonians, who in 586 B.C. razed the Jews' house of worship, the First Temple, in Jerusalem. Their homeland occupied, the Jews of Israel faced the bitter prospect of wandering endlessly on its periphery.

The Jews' adversity only strengthened their faith in Yahweh, their commitment to live in accordance with the Torah, and their certainty that someday they would reclaim their rightful home. Their dreams materialized in 538 B.C. when the Persians invaded Israel and, after ousting the Babylonian forces there, allowed the Jews to return. Gladdened by this homecoming, they entered a period of spiritual revival, vowing an even stricter adherence to the Mosaic Code and replacing their demolished temple with a second one.

Roman soldiers plunder Jerusalem's Second Temple in this relief from the Arch of Titus, erected in A.D. 81 to honor the Roman emperor who conquered the Jews.

The Diaspora

Defeat came again, however, at the hands of the Romans, whose imperial ambitions had driven them east to the land of the Israelites, which became a Roman province called Palestine. The Romans first maintained a small army near Jerusalem, then launched a full-scale invasion and forcibly entered the city, destroying the Second Temple in A.D. 70. In A.D. 135, the Romans officially outlawed Judaism and ordered the Jews of Palestine to disperse throughout the Roman world.

French Jews of the 12th century illustrated this edition of the Mishna, a codification of Jewish law included in the Talmud.

This dispersal—or Diaspora—had two important consequences. First, Jews directed their energies away from establishing a homeland and focused instead on scholarly aims, applying themselves to an intense study of their holy books. Second, Judaic thought and culture spread to the far-flung corners of the Roman Empire—Europe, North Africa, and the Levant (the countries bordering the eastern part of the Mediterranean Sea).

Before long, Jews made up about one-tenth of the population of the Roman Empire. In fact, even a few important Roman officials converted to Judaism despite the Roman ban on the religion and despite the fact that the waning empire adopted Christianity as its official religion after A.D. 313.

From the distance of 2,000 years, it may look as though the Jews practiced a uniform creed before the Roman invasion. But Judaism was not always a single, unified faith. Various sects, some of which contradicted the teachings of Judaism, sprang up under charismatic leaders. One such leader, Jesus Christ, expounded a philosophy based on many precepts of Judaic thought. His followers accepted him as the Messiah (the name *Jesus Christ* is a translation from classical Greek of *Joshua the Messiah*), and his teachings gained enormous influence, forming the basis of the Christian faith.

Secure in the sanctuary of their homeland, Jews freely disagreed among themselves. But exile thrust them into different lands with competing theologies, and their differences mended. Jews devoted themselves to the practice of Judaism with renewed fervor; their beliefs took on a more uniform cast. The vast majority of Jews were separated by thousands of miles from their homeland—which was now called Palestine by the Romans to eliminate its identity with the Israelites—but Judaism endured. Although a significant number of Jews continued to live in the ancient homeland, in the area near the Sea of Galilee, most Jews were completely cut off from them.

Across Europe

Dispersed throughout foreign, often hostile, lands, Jews faced anti-Semitism so extreme that it menaced their survival as a people. Many Christians blamed Jews for killing Jesus Christ, when in fact Jews and Romans together—alarmed by Christ's growing power in Jerusalem—had conspired to end his life. Christians reacted by identifying Jews as the "Antichrist" and outlawing Judaism in parts of the Middle East and Europe, where many transplanted Jews had settled. In order to break the Jews' spirit, Europeans burned their synagogues and settlements during much of the first millennium A.D.

Yet somehow Judaism thrived. Generations of rabbis, scholars, and laymen studied the Torah meticulously, and the body of their commentary grew into the Talmud, a codification of Jewish law, encyclopedic in scope, set down in the 5th century and repeatedly refined and reinterpreted. In such centers of Jewish life as Mesopotamia, Spain, and (later) the Rhineland, experts on Jewish law guided other Jews on civic as well as spiritual matters.

As the years passed, Jews fanned out across North Africa and most of Europe. They did not again constitute a majority of any nation's population, as they had in their own homeland, but they made their presence felt. In Spain, for example, where Jews flourished from the 9th through the 15th centuries, a Jewish literary revival took root and enriched the national culture. Spain's tolerance of Jews had no equal in medieval Europe. In other countries, virtually all power and wealth belonged to the aristocracy and to the Catholic church, leaving Jews without a voice. Moreover, laws denied Jews the right to own land and to enter most professions.

In the 10th and 11th centuries, trade and commerce began to grow in Europe. Merchants from cities in France and Italy journeyed all the way to the Orient to obtain silks and spices. These adventurous traders included Jews, whose dispersal provided them with an international network of potential business partners who spoke the same language and shared the same beliefs. This network seemed the perfect means for the Jews to establish an independent trade route, one that would enable them to compete in the marketplace.

But once again, Jews found their hands tied, this time by powerful Gentile merchants who barred Jews from trading. At this point, nearly every occupation was closed to them. In desperation, Jews flocked to one of the few open professions: finance. The mercantile economy of the late Middle Ages depended on money to grease the wheels of trade, but the Catholic church frowned on moneylending as a vice fit only for infidels. Naturally, no objection was raised when Jews stepped in to fill the role of banker.

Meanwhile, bigotry continued its march throughout Europe. Jews were banished from England in 1290, from France in 1394, and from Spain in 1492. During the 300-year reign of terror now known as the Spanish Inquisition, hundreds of thousands of Jews who refused to convert to Catholicism were burned alive, tortured, or locked in dungeons. In German territories, expulsion of the Jewish population followed a series of massacres. There, as in Spain, some Jews professed belief in Catholicism in order to save their lives; others actually converted; and many chose to die rather than renounce their faith. The Germans burned Jewish books and desecrated synagogues, acts that were repeated by the Nazis in the 20th century.

In the 15th and 16th centuries, Poland alone provided a safe haven for Jews, especially for those driven eastward from Germany. Polish leaders took the radical step of introducing rights for Jews into the country's legal code and also protected their commercial activities. The Jews who became permanent residents of Poland came to be known as Ashkenazim, a name derived from the Hebrew word for Germany. By the late 1930s, when World War II began, Poland had more Jews than any other European country—about 3 million. During the war, German Nazis destroyed nearly half of Europe's Jewish population by rounding up the Jews who lived in Poland.

Generally, Jews of the 15th and 16th centuries fared better in countries with Islamic rulers than they did in Christian ones. Turkey, for instance, granted entry to many victims of the Diaspora. Later, during the Spanish Inquisition, the Turkish Ottoman Empire opened its doors to Sephardim—Jews from Spain—an acceptance that proved both a blessing and a curse. In Turkey, Jews gained more freedom than they had known in Europe. Yet as they intermingled with the Muslim majority, their religion became diluted with elements of Islamic mysticism.

Some Jews responded to this unwanted influence by migrating back to Palestine, which was now part of the Turkish Ottoman Empire, contributing to the growth of the Jewish population in Palestine. Eastern European Jews who went to Palestine bought land from Arab landlords, drained swamps, and founded settlements. By the middle of the 19th century, the majority of Jerusalem's population was Jewish. Other Jews migrated to northern

A miniature from a 13th-century European Bible depicts King Solomon reading from the Torah.

Baron James de Rothschild (1792–1868), who made his home in France, often used his considerable influence with that country's government to aid fellow Jews at home and abroad.

Europe, especially to Hamburg, Germany, to London, England, and to Amsterdam, Holland. These cities had become centers of the Protestant branch of Christianity, and Jews in Protestant Europe had greater freedom than those in Catholic lands to worship and conduct business as they chose.

These cities gave rise to a new phenomenon, the Westernized Jew. Earlier European Jews had managed to retain their faith because they were exposed to no rival religions and came into contact with other Jews. Now that they could move freely in society, Jews of northern Europe longed to participate in the wider secular world but were excluded from it by their own tradition and philosophy. Many felt torn between their devotion to Judaism and their desire to sample the pleasures of a cosmopolitan life.

A new era for the rights of Jews (as for many others) loomed in 1789, when the French Revolution introduced liberal values that traveled throughout the Continent. By the mid-19th century Jews had won political emancipation in most of western Europe, and in 1858 the first Jew gained a seat in England's Parliament. The new liberal climate fostered the advancement of numerous Jews, most notably the Rothschilds, a family of financiers. Other Jews became prominent artists, scientists, and statesmen, though such success entailed compromise—Britain's prime minister Benjamin Disraeli, for example, expediently converted to Christianity early in his life. As religious tolerance increased, it eroded the cultural and social boundaries that had always divided Jews and Gentiles. In many western European cities, ghettos vanished, their residents free to live wherever they pleased.

Progress marked Jewish life in France, England, Germany, and Holland, but the 4 million Jews of eastern Europe never enjoyed the rights of full citizenship. In 1880, nearly half of world Jewry was isolated inside the Pale of Settlement—an area of eastern Poland and western Russia to which all the Jews of the region had been consigned. These Jews usually lived in isolated and impoverished villages or shtetls. This insularity served the Jews well, however, first by spawning a vibrant Jewish culture and second by leaving Jews relatively free from direct intervention in their daily lives.

During the 18th century, Polish shtetls gave birth to the popular Orthodox movement practiced by the Hasidim (Hebrew for "pious ones"). Hasidic rabbis railed against the tradition of scholarship within Judaism. They argued that God wanted Jews to believe with their hearts—not their minds. The Hasidim practiced an emotional, almost ecstatic type of prayer that they believed would afford them direct connection with God. In order to distinguish themselves from the other Jews around them, Hasidic men adopted the style of dress of Polish noblemen; even today they wear long black coats. At its peak, Hasidism claimed followers among roughly half of Europe's Jews.

Although Hasidim and other Jews of eastern Europe remained sequestered within the Pale, their mere presence riled Gentile authorities. Also in 1648 marauding Cossacks—cavalrymen in the czar's army—killed 100,000 Jews, and similar butchery continued for the next 250 years. Continous waves of massacres—or *pogroms*—kept Jews in a state of constant terror. The killers justified their deeds first as a religious obligation

(Jews, they argued, posed a threat to the mother church of Russia) and then as a racial one (Jews were not Slavs). This prolonged persecution, which climaxed in 1881 and again in 1904, drove millions of Jews to leave their "nation" for America between 1880 and 1920.

Many Jews were moved to emigrate by the action of two powerful forces. On one hand, they were pushed into emigrating by problems in their home countries; such problems included poverty, overcrowding (the Pale experienced a sharp rise in population during the 19th century), limited opportunities, and persecution and oppression. At the same time, however, emigrants were also pulled to America by the ideals of freedom and opportunity. America offered more than just a chance to escape the problems of home. It also attracted emigrants with the image of a country that gave everyone who was willing to work, no matter how poor or uneducated, the

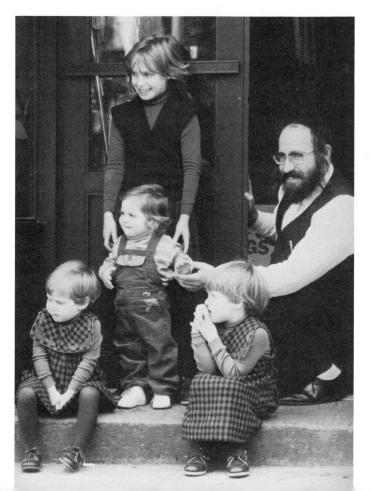

Today, Hasidic Jews in America generally live in urban neighborhoods such as Williamsburg in Brooklyn, New York.

chance to go to free public schools and to advance in a climate of political, economic, and religious freedom unknown elsewhere in the world. Yet America was not the goal of every Jew who thought about emigrating. Some dreamed of a Jewish homeland.

Oppression rekindled the Jews' desire for a homeland. One Jew in particular, Theodor Herzl, a Hungarian, argued that the only remedy for persecution was for Jews to establish an independent state in Palestine. Toward that end he organized a formal movement, called Zionism, and in 1896 published a highly influential pamphlet, *The Jewish State*. The following year, Herzl convened the first World Zionist Congress, in Basel, Switzerland. His efforts won much support, but a majority of the Jewish population found the prospect of a Jewish state hopelessly unrealistic: Palestine, after all, remained a part of the Turkish Ottoman Empire.

Turkey sided with Germany in World War I (1914–18), and when Germany lost the war, Turkey also was defeated. The Ottoman Empire, long plagued by corruption, finally disintegrated. The League of Nations—a forerunner of the United Nations—assumed control of territories that had been under Ottoman rule for centuries. The League gave Palestine and Iraq to Britain to administer, while France received Syria and Lebanon. In the 1920s, the British set up an Arab state called Transjordan (now known as Jordan) in the part of Palestine that was east of the Jordan River, but they continued to govern the western part. The British did not allow many Jews to immigrate into Palestine during the 1920s, 1930s, and 1940s, not even to escape the Holocaust— the great slaughter of the Jews of Europe by the Nazis during World War II. To Zionists, the Holocaust was the final, bitter proof that they were right: the Jews needed a country of their own to protect themselves. Zionists in Palestine clamored for independence and carried on a terrorist campaign against the British, who in 1947 gave up and turned the territory over to the United Nations.

The United Nations devised a compromise that was intended to satisfy the competing claims of both the Jews, who felt that their claim to Palestine dated from ancient times, and the Arabs, who had been living in Palestine ever since the Islamic conquest of the 6th century. In 1948, Palestine was partitioned, or divided; the part of the territory where most of the Palestinian Arabs lived was granted to the Arabs, and the part where most of the Palestinian Jews lived was granted to the Jews for the formation of a Jewish state. In 1948, nearly 2,000 years after the Jews were expelled from their homeland by the Romans, and half a century after Herzl's first Zionist Congress, the modern state of Israel was born. The Arab nations surrounding Israel, however, were opposed to the establishment of a Jewish state in the area. The conflict between Israel, its Arab neighbors, and the Palestinian Arabs living in Israeli-controlled territory has led to several wars; that conflict continues today, although there have been some steps toward peace.

Folkways

When Zionism first gained broad popularity, some eastern European Jews set out for the deserts and swamps of western Palestine, a largely unoccupied area of what would someday become modern Israel. There they purchased land from Arab owners and founded settlements. Most, however, chose another route away from the hardships of the Pale and embarked for America, bring-

Theodor Herzl sits in the foreground of a group portrait photographed aboard a boat bound for Palestine.

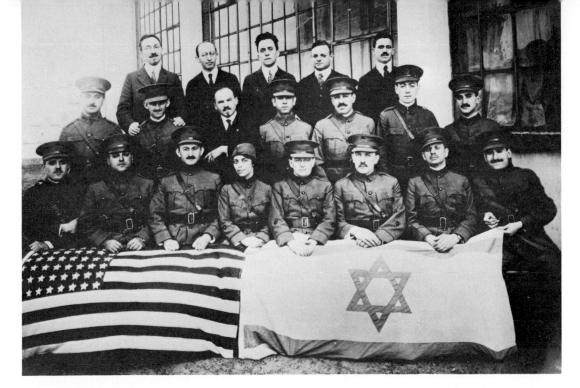

ing with them traditional customs and a unique, hybrid language—Yiddish. Yiddish had its origins in the 10th century, when Jews from northern France settled along the Rhine River, absorbing German into their own vocabulary but writing it with the Hebrew alphabet. As the language evolved, about 70 percent of its words came directly from German, another 10 percent originated in Hebrew, and the rest filtered in from the native tongues of countries where Jews had settled. By World War II some 11 million Jews worldwide could understand Yiddish.

Most American-born Jews of the 20th century have abandoned the use of Yiddish, but recent concern that the language will disappear has sparked a modest Yiddish revival. Similarly, American Jews, and especially young adults, have shown increased interest in preserving the traditional Judaism practiced by grandparents and great-grandparents in the Old World.

Since their days in the deserts of Canaan, Jews have observed special dietary laws (called *kashrut*) set forth in the Old Testament. Their meat must come from animals that chew their cud and have cloven hooves (such as the cow and sheep), and their fish must have scales

Many American Jews, such as the members of this volunteer medical corps stationed in Palestine, have supported the Zionist movement since its earliest days.

and fins. One passage from Leviticus lists some of the foods forbidden to them:

> These also shall be unclean unto you among the
> creeping things that creep upon the earth; the weasel,
> and the mouse, and the tortoise after his kind,
> And the ferret, and the chameleon, and the lizard, and
> the snail, and the mole.

In antiquity, such restrictions probably served as a kind of public health code. Certain foods still not allowed under kashrut reflect the ancient concern with healthfulness: pork, a known carrier of trichinosis, and shellfish, often tainted with hepatitis, are prohibited by Jewish dietary law. Even foods that are *kosher*, or ritually correct, require special preparation under kashrut. Meats, unless boiled, must be cleansed with coarse salt and then soaked to remove all traces of blood. Meat and dairy products must be eaten separately and served with different sets of dishes.

Contemporary Jews do not universally observe the laws of kashrut, but the vast majority continue to celebrate the special holidays of Judaism. Many of these commemorate the cornerstones of Jewish history. During the yearly springtime feast of Passover, Jews reflect on the Exodus from Egypt and give thanks for their freedom. Most Christians probably do not realize that the Last Supper of Jesus Christ was in fact a *seder*, or Passover meal.

During December, the time of the winter solstice, Jews celebrate Hanukkah, the Festival of Lights, by giving gifts and lighting candles in a candelabra known as a *menorah*. The candles in the Hanukkah menorah represent eight miraculous days in which an oil lamp that contained enough fuel for only a single night, burned for seven more, illuminating Jerusalem's Second Temple.

The holiest time of year for Jews occurs in early autumn, the beginning of the Hebrew calendar year. Jewish "high holy days" commence with the New

Year's celebration of Rosh Hashanah, an occasion marking the date on which—according to Jewish tradition—the world was created. Jews consider this a happy but solemn occasion, a time of self-scrutiny, when God passes annual judgment on his children. The contemplative mood of Rosh Hashanah intensifies during the most sacred day of the year, Yom Kippur (the Day of Atonement), observed by Jews with fasting and prayer. The ritual celebration of holidays such as Passover, Hanukkah, Rosh Hashanah, and Yom Kippur has kept Judaism alive throughout history and certainly sustained generations of Jews who immigrated to the alien lands of North America. 〜

WAVES OF IMMIGRATION

Nearly 2,000 Jews lived in the 13 colonies when the Declaration of Independence was signed in 1776. The history of Jewish Americans, however, began more than a century earlier, in September 1654. At the time, New York was still the Dutch colony of New Amsterdam, and Peter Stuyvesant was its governor. The city's latest arrivals included a group of 23 Jewish men, women, and children, refugees from Dutch Brazil. This land had recently been reconquered by its first colonists, the Portuguese, who refused to allow Jews in their territories.

The 23 Jews anticipated a warm reception in New Amsterdam, for its parent nation, Holland, had shown remarkable tolerance toward them. The Dutch capital, Amsterdam, housed a large Jewish community, one of the most vital in Europe. But in New Amsterdam the the Brazilian refugees got a chilly reception from Governor Stuyvesant, who had no fondness for religious dissenters. He wrote his employers, the Dutch West India Company, requesting permission to expel the newcomers in order that "the deceitful race,—such hateful enemies and blasphemers of the name of Christ,—be not allowed further to infect and trouble this new colony."

But Jews have always been good at organizing and lobbying. Back in Amsterdam, the Jewish community put pressure on the Dutch West India Company, which was responsible for much colonizing in North America. Jews argued that the New World still had plenty of room, that settlers were needed, and that more colonists meant increased revenue from trade and taxes. But it was probably an altogether different argument that hit a responsive nerve: "Your Honors should also please consider that many of the Jewish nation are principal shareholders in the Company." The company wrote back to New Amsterdam ordering Stuyvesant to let the Jews stay.

Over the next two centuries, the Jewish-American population grew slowly but steadily. In the 17th and 18th centuries, a significant number of Jews lived in Dutch and British colonies in the Caribbean and South America, and some of them eventually migrated to the North American colonies. Charleston, South Carolina, and Savannah, Georgia, had populations of Sephardic Jews in colonial times. The Jewish population of North America numbered perhaps 2,000 when the American Revolution ended in 1783. By that time synagogues had

Uriah Philips Levy, the first Jewish American to obtain the rank of commodore in the United States Navy, fought in the War of 1812.

been established in New York, Newport, Savannah, Philadelphia, and Charleston.

Jews showed their gratitude to their fellow colonists by taking an active part in the revolutionary war, both as soldiers and as suppliers for Washington's army. One of the Revolution's financiers was Haym Solomon, a Jew who first sold bonds and then expended all his own resources for the colonists' cause. And in 1790 a local newspaper printed correspondence between George Washington and the Jewish community of Newport, Rhode Island, the site of America's oldest temple, Touro Synagogue. The new president assured this enclave that the American government "gives to bigotry no sanction." Also, the Jews could rejoice when Article VI of the new Constitution ensured that "no religious test shall ever be required as a qualification to any office or public trust." The First Amendment proclaimed further that "Congress shall make no law respecting an establishment of religion, or prohibiting the free exercise thereof." To a population whose history consisted of almost uninterrupted persecution, these seemed magnificent guarantees. As a Philadelphia observer noted during a celebration for the new Constitution, "The rabbi of the Jews, locked in the arms of two ministers of the gospel, was a most delightful sight."

Despite America's tolerant laws, Jews hesitated to immigrate to the new country. During the first half century of the Republic, its Jewish population grew by only a few thousand. Jews held back in part because of the French Revolution. It occurred only a decade later than America's and offered Jews hope for a better life on a continent that, unlike North America, was familiar to them. Optimism grew in 1791, when France's National Assembly granted rights of citizenship to Jews.

But the outlook dimmed after the defeat of the French emperor Napoleon in the early 1800s. Throughout Europe, reactionary forces immediately attempted to turn back the clock. Jews lost most of the gains they had recently achieved, and a rash of anti-Semitic acts swept the Continent. For instance, the German king-

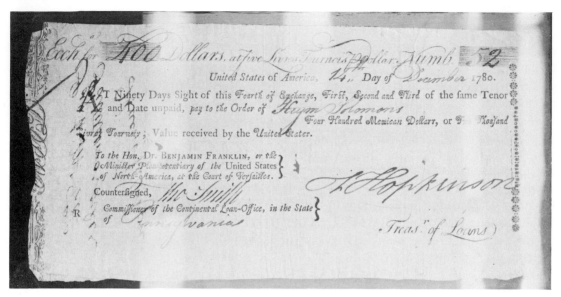

In 1780, the United States issued this bank note to Haym Salomon, a Polish-born Jew who helped finance the American Revolution.

dom of Bavaria (where Adolf Hitler launched his career a century later) oppressed Jews with burdensome taxes and with humiliating restrictions on the work they could perform and the places they could live. Authorities even imposed obstacles to marriage. The failure of a liberal uprising that took place in several German states (and swept across Europe) in 1848 also spurred tens of thousands of Germans, Jews among them, to emigrate.

The numbers tell the story. In 1830 about 6,000 Jews lived in the United States; most of them spoke English and had been born in the New World. Thirty years later, the Jewish-American population numbered 150,000, and the community largely spoke German. By 1880 the count had risen to 250,000, including the first wave of Yiddish-speaking Jews from eastern Europe. The leap from 6,000 to 250,000, though impressive, only hinted at what was to come. By 1920, the number of Jewish Americans reached *4 million*, the largest Jewish population in the world.

In 1880, an equivalent number (and half the world's Jews at the time) lived in the Russian Empire, restricted to the Pale of Settlement. Conditions there were miserable. Aside from the poverty of the shtetls and the outbreaks of government-sanctioned violence, Jews suffered from an unjust system of military conscription that forced Jewish men—sometimes boys as young as 12—to serve in the czar's army for as long as 25 years.

When Alexander II became czar in 1855, he initiated a series of mild reforms. But in 1881 he was assassinated by a terrorist bomb, and the regime that succeeded him stepped up hostilities against Jews. It passed anti-Semitic laws and permitted a series of pogroms—more than 200 in 1881 and 1882. A newspaper called the *Jewish Chronicle* described the horrors of one of the 1881 Moscow pogroms:

> Four thousand Jewish families are in utter destitution, through the pillage of three whole days; sixteen persons have been murdered; sixty seriously wounded; females have been brutally violated; a mother, who was trying to prevent her daughter from being outraged, had her ears cut off and died from loss of blood; Jewish synagogues have been pillaged; the books of the Law torn and trodden upon.

Faced with such terrorism, more than one-third of Russia's Jews emigrated, more than 90 percent of them bound for America. They were joined by Jews from the Austro-Hungarian Empire, where local conditions were often grim, and from Romania, where life was as bad as it was in the Pale. Although these thousands of emigrants

An 1848 engraving depicts the struggle between German revolutionaries and the national parliament.

shared a common faith, there was great diversity among them. Jews who came from different regions and states of Europe were as culturally, socially, and politically diverse as non-Jews from the same points of origin.

The trek to freedom was an ordeal. First of all, immigrants had to save enough money to make the journey—no easy task for those living in poverty. Next, they had to get to one of the European port cities, such as Hamburg or Amsterdam. The journey might involve stealing across a border; any draftable young Russian men discovered by the border authorities were collared and delivered to the army. Most of the immigrants had little or no urban experience. When they found themselves in big, unfamiliar cities, they were frightened and disoriented—perfect prey for cheaters and hucksters with reassuring smiles, ready to rob them of every penny.

Immigration often involved the separation of families. Many husbands, sons, and fathers came to America alone, planning to work and save money so that they could bring their parents, siblings, or wives and children to join them. Sometimes years passed before families were reunited.

For the immigrants of the early 19th century, the voyage across the Atlantic Ocean lasted several weeks. Most

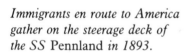

Immigrants en route to America gather on the steerage deck of the SS Pennland *in 1893.*

immigrants traveled in steerage, paying the cheapest rates for a place in the area under the deck, massed together in squalor and stench. Seasickness was a constant misery. The voyage was shorter and less miserable after the introduction of steam-powered ships in the 1860s. By the end of the century, steamships had replaced sailing ships, and immigrants crossed the ocean in seven to ten days.

Immigrants entered the United States at many ports. Some came to Philadelphia, Baltimore, Boston, or Galveston, Texas. The biggest and busiest port of entry on the East Coast, however, was Ellis Island in New York Harbor, opened in 1892. Here the immigrants, many of whom were already exhausted from the strain of leaving home and the rigors of the voyage, were examined to make sure that they met the qualifications for entering the country. Doctors checked them for signs of tuberculosis and other diseases. Officials asked them whether they had money to live on, jobs lined up, and people waiting to meet them. Some immigrants remained at the immigration stations for a week or even longer, waiting to receive clearance to enter the United States.

A public health official on Ellis Island examines a woman's eyes for signs of disease, around 1900.

The trauma of Ellis Island was eased by organizations that American Jews had set up to help the immigrants. The best known and most successful was the Hebrew Immigrant Aid Society (HIAS), one of the first such organizations established by the eastern European Jews themselves rather than their German-Jewish predecessors. HIAS staff members acted as interpreters and mediators between government officials and the new arrivals. They gave the immigrants practical advice about life in the New World and protected them from sharpers and swindlers. They pressured the steamship companies to improve conditions in steerage; later on, they lobbied Congress against laws restricting immigration. Finally, the HIAS helped the new immigrants find jobs and even provided shelter for them.

From Ellis Island, most of the newcomers made their way into the slums and sweatshops of New York or other large American cities. The trip was over, and the days that ensued were hard, but hardship was something Jews had known for centuries. The flood from eastern Europe continued to increase as the new immigrants made a life for themselves and then sent for their families. At the turn of the century the Jewish community in the United States had grown to about 1 million. By 1910 it exceeded 2 million; by 1914 it had reached nearly 3 million; 10 years after that the number was approximately 4 million.

World War I brought immigration to a temporary halt. Immigration picked up again briefly after the end of the war in 1918, but by the 1920s America's hospitality was waning. In the aftermath of the war, the country adopted a policy of isolationism that was based, in part, on a widespread distrust of foreigners. Americans were troubled by new social and cultural fears; they worried that new immigrants such as the Jews were not assimilating into mainstream society, and that unchecked immigration would create foreign subcultures within America. In particular, anti-Semitism spread alarmingly in the United States during these years (although not as alarmingly as it did in Europe). In 1921, 1924, and 1927 the U.S. Congress passed laws to limit immigration. The flood of newcomers dwindled to a trickle.

It picked up force again in the mid-1930s, when Jewish refugees from Hitler's Germany began arriving. These men and women came from backgrounds that differed markedly from those of the poor, unskilled eastern European immigrants of the previous half century. Most German refugees could afford to flee, and three-quarters of them were past the age of 40. They included lawyers, doctors, and merchants as well as brilliant scientists (including Albert Einstein), psychologists, scholars, writers, and artists. The 150,000 who came between 1935 and 1941 composed a large enough community for Manhattan's West Side—where most of the émigrés lived—to be nicknamed "the Fourth Reich."

World War II (1939–45) led to one of the saddest chapters in Jewish immigration. Despite the brutal treat-

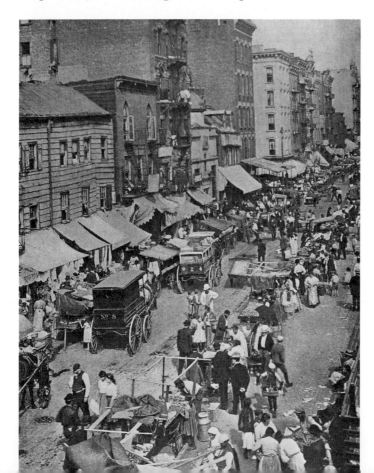

In 1889, Hester Street was home to thousands of Jewish immigrants on New York City's Lower East Side.

ment of European Jews by the Nazis, the U.S. Congress stubbornly refused to relax immigration quotas, and the State Department put up one obstacle after another for Jews seeking residence in the United States. At the same time, Jews had great difficulty getting into British-controlled Palestine because some members of the British government were anti-Semitic, and also because Arab officials in Palestine were hostile toward Jewish immigrants. Jewish leaders appealed to U.S. president Franklin D. Roosevelt to pressure Britain into letting more refugees into Palestine, but the U.S. government did very little. It even refused to bomb the gas chambers at Auschwitz—a concentration camp where thousands of Jews were killed by the Nazis—because it regarded such activity as a diversion from the task of winning the war.

In recent decades, Jewish newcomers to America have arrived mainly from three countries: Iran, Israel, and the Soviet Union. In 1979, the shah of Iran was overthrown. The new Islamic fundamentalist government, under the leadership of the Ayatollah Ruhollah Khomeini, imprisoned or executed many members of the small Jewish population. Most of the rest eventually fled, including many who reached this country. America has also received a steady stream of immigrants from Israel. Some of these men and women found conditions too harsh in the Jewish state; others disliked living under the constant threat of war. Some simply viewed the United States the way Jews have for the last two centuries: as the land of opportunity.

The former Soviet Union, with its roughly 2 million Jews, has the third-largest Jewish population in the world today, after the United States and Israel. But anti-Semitism there has never died out. The Soviet government made life hard for Jews and also made it difficult for them to emigrate. Nevertheless—owing in part, no doubt, to pressure from the American government and in turn, from American Jews—more than a quarter of a million Russian Jews have been allowed to emigrate over the last couple of decades, and many have made their way to the United States.

Canadian Jews

In some aspects—most notably in its immigration history—the story of the Jews in Canada parallels that of Jews in the United States; but Judaism in Canada has developed its own distinct history. The date marking the first Jewish settlement there can be fixed precisely: 1759, the same year the British conquered the colony of New France. Until then, Jews had been barred by the French from France's North American territory in what is now Canada. Canadian Jews responded gratefully to British tolerance, repaying the favor with unwavering loyalty to the redcoats during the American Revolution in 1776. Later, during the War of 1812, Canadian Jews again supported the British against the

Americans, despite strong family ties to Jews living in the new Republic.

Throughout the 19th century the British continued their tolerant treatment of Canadian Jews. In 1832 Jews received full civil rights, a privilege not yet enjoyed by Jews in the mother country of England. By 1867, when the provinces of Ontario, Quebec, New Brunswick, and Nova Scotia banded together to form the Dominion of Canada, about a thousand Jews lived in Canada, mainly in Montreal, Quebec City, Kingston, Toronto, and Hamilton. Most of these settlers traced their origins to western and central Europe.

The tidal wave of eastern European immigration that dramatically changed the face of Jewry in the United States also swept across Canada. By 1881 about 2,400 Jews had migrated there; by 1891 the figure had risen to 6,400; and by 1921, Canada's Jewish population had swelled to more than 126,000. Most immigrants made their new homes in Montreal and Toronto, gathering in dense, close-knit ghettos, as they did in so many cities in the United States.

Unlike their U.S. counterparts, however, Canadian Jews quickly moved westward—by 1920 the city of Winnipeg in the prairie province of Manitoba had the third-largest Jewish population in the country. Canada could also claim its share of Jewish farmers. The earliest eastern European immigrants had shown little talent for working the land, but with the help of the Jewish Colonization Association, Jews established farms in the provinces of Manitoba, Saskatchewan, Alberta, and, after World War I, in Ontario.

During World War II, Canada responded to the plight of European Jews with an indifference equal to America's. Canada remained all but closed to refugees: Between 1933 and 1945, fewer than 5,000 Jews were admitted, and after the holocaust Canada found room for only 8,000 additional survivors. When asked how many Jews would be allowed into Canada after the war, one Canadian official told a group of journalists: "None

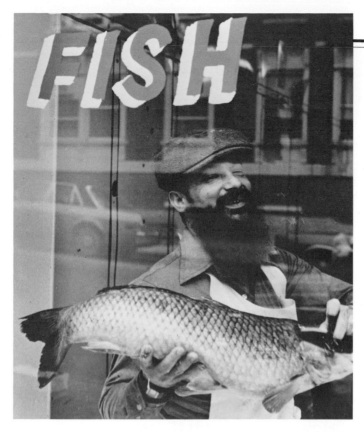

is too many." For the first time since it had officially accepted Jews, Canada seemed to be swayed by the anti-Semitism endemic in Europe. And alarmed Jewish citizens noticed an increased hostility in their countrymen.

Canadian Jews were relieved when this sudden malice receded at the war's end, and Jewish immigration picked up shortly thereafter. After the failure of the 1956 anticommunist uprising in Hungary, Canada accepted thousands of Hungarian refugees, including 4,500 Jews. The later part of the decade saw the beginnings of an influx of French-speaking Jews from Morocco and other North African countries; these immigrants found a congenial welcome in French-speaking Quebec. In recent years, Canada has become home to Jewish refugees from the former Soviet Union, who today number among the nation's more than 300,000 Jews—the sixth-largest Jewish population in the world. ❧

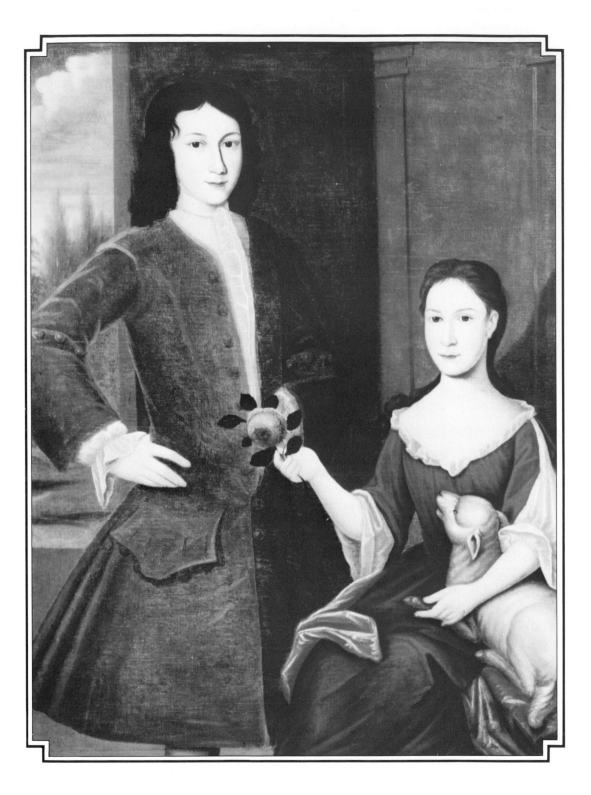

LIFE IN AMERICA

For centuries, anti-Semitic laws in Europe had barred Jews from nearly every profession except commerce. They were prohibited from owning land—the principal source of wealth in agrarian society—and restricted also from becoming artisans because the medieval craft guilds denied them membership. Through necessity, Jews took on the roles of merchant and moneylender. These vocations also sustained them in America. As a 1738 observer in Georgia noted of the German-Jewish immigrants there, "They have no other profession besides farming or dealing in small trade. The latter comes easier to them than the former."

Although most Americans tilled the "fruited plains" to make their living, Jewish-American farmers were a rare sight in the 18th century. In the next two centuries many Jews tried vainly to set up agricultural communities in the United States, but the majority failed dismally. Not until recently—when Israelis developed the cooperative farms known as *kibbutzim* and performed miracles of irrigation in the Middle Eastern desert—did Jews show any aptitude for working the land.

But they did have a knack for commerce. Long before the American Revolution, Jewish merchants had established successful stores in New York, Newport, Savannah, Philadelphia, and Charleston. Soon the commercial ties between Jews were strengthened by family

Many 19th-century German immigrants peddled household goods across America, traveling either by foot or with a horse and wagon.

alliances as the sons and daughters of wealthy merchants married one another. Such unions benefited immigrant Jews not only economically but also culturally, helping Jewish families retain their identity. In a land where the Jewish population was small—and where intermingling with Gentiles was unavoidable—Jews worried that their people would eventually disappear into the American melting pot.

The challenge of maintaining Jewish identity was most pronounced in small towns. Many early immigrants, eager to fit into American society, grew lax about such fundamental religious duties as keeping kosher households and observing the Jewish Sabbath, which falls on Saturday. In 1791, a woman in Petersburg, Virginia, wrote to her parents in Germany:

> I know quite well you will not want me to bring up my children like Gentiles. Here they cannot become anything else. Jewishness is pushed aside. . . . On the Sabbath all the Jewish shops are open; and they do business on that day as they do throughout the week.

Although this woman enjoyed small-town life in the United States—"You cannot know what a wonderful country this is for the common man"—she decided she must move to a city.

Jews from Germany

Beginning in 1830, anxieties about assimilation waned as German-Jewish immigrants flowed into the United States. Families from Germany typically migrated in several stages: a single family member, usually a son, came to America and saved sufficient earnings to bring over first one relative, then another. Most of these young immigrants took up peddling and supplied an expanding America with a host of sorely needed goods. As a rising number of Americans left the East Coast and ventured into wilderness territory they left behind the luxury of stores, usually shopping in town only once or twice a year. Thus, the peddler's cart was always a welcome sight. For their part, immigrants gravitated

In about 1890, employees pose in front of S. Lazarus & Company—a Columbus, Ohio, department store founded by Jewish Americans.

toward peddling because they could purchase their first bundle of goods on credit. Their packs, often weighing as much as 120 pounds, seemed backbreaking. "The walking of from ten to twenty miles per day I did not relish," one recalled dryly. Another noted in his journal:

> It is hard, very hard indeed, to make a living this way.
> Sweat runs down my body in great drops and my
> back seems to be breaking, but I cannot stop. . . .
> Each day I must ask and importune some farmer's wife
> to buy my wares, a few pennies' worth. Accursed
> desire for money, it is you that has driven the Bavarian
> immigrants to this wretched kind of trade!

German Jews quickly won a place in the American economy. The formula "from pack-on-back to store to department store" seems an exaggeration, but it accurately described the rapid climb many German-Jewish immigrants made up the financial ladder. And some farsighted entrepreneurs used their peddler's packs to lay the groundwork for businesses that grew into retail empires. Macy's and Gimbels in New York; F. & R. Lazarus in Columbus, Ohio; Filene's in Boston; Thalhimer Bros. in Richmond; Meier & Frank in Portland, Oregon—all had Jewish founders. Estée Lauder and Helena Rubinstein, in cosmetics, were two successful Jewish women who started out small, as was Lena (Lane) Bryant in fashion. Jews also moved successfully into meat packing, investment banking, and clothing manufacture.

The best-known clothing manufacturer was Levi Strauss, a Bavarian Jew who immigrated to this country in 1848, at the age of 17. In New York, he paid his dues as a peddler before accumulating enough capital to head for San Francisco. According to legend, he met a gold prospector there who glanced at the heavy fabric Strauss had brought with him and remarked, "You should have brought pants"—apparently mining was

By 1870, Levi Strauss had established himself as a successful merchant of ready-to-wear clothing.

rough on that particular item of clothing. The actual story is more complicated. A shrewd merchant, Strauss had already built up a flourishing San Francisco dry-goods business by 1872, when he received a letter from a Russian Jewish tailor living in Reno, Nevada, who had designed some heavy trousers from denim he had purchased from Levi Strauss & Co.: "The secret of them Pents is the Rivits that I put in those Pockets and I found the demand so large that I cannot make them up fast enough." Strauss must have been impressed,

A German-Jewish New Year's card from 1910 depicts an elegant holiday dinner.

because he decided to form a partnership with the tailor, procuring a patent to make "Levi's." Today Levi Strauss & Co. is a major manufacturing corporation, still centered in San Francisco and directed by Levi Strauss's heirs.

Other Jewish peddlers made their way to Cincinnati via Ohio River trade routes and built bustling shopping districts. These peddlers also erected garment factories—a natural extension of their retail businesses—and turned Cincinnati into a major center of clothing manufacture. This industry spawned a large, wealthy Jewish community, which founded the first American seminary for rabbinical training, Hebrew Union College.

A New Type of Immigrant

By 1880, Jewish Americans could feel extremely satisfied. They had achieved economic success; they had merged easily into American society; they had won the respect of their Gentile neighbors. But the situation suddenly changed. From 1880 to the mid-1920s, heavy waves of immigration swelled the country's Jewish population from 250,000 to more than 4 million.

The assimilated German Jews gazed uneasily on the mass migration. They had worked hard to combat the old Jewish stereotypes and to gain acceptance. Would all their progress be negated by invading hordes of eastern European paupers who appeared peculiar to American eyes, practiced Orthodox Judaism (in contrast to the more worldly Reform Judaism of the Germans), and seemed bumpkins hopelessly unprepared for America's big cities? Critical though they tended to be, some German Jews went to great lengths to ease the lives of the newcomers. They fought federal legislation that would have restricted immigration, and many Jewish philanthropic organizations got their start when German Jews reached out to help impoverished Russian Jews by establishing schools, libraries, and hospitals.

In New York, the "downtown" east Europeans on Manhattan's Lower East Side and the "uptown" Germans on the Upper West Side carried on a stormy relationship for decades; one uptown paper, finding the downtowners "slovenly in dress, loud in manners, and vulgar in discourse," declared that they had to "be

An eastern European immigrant prepares for the Sabbath in a coal cellar on Ludlow Street on the Lower East Side of New York City.

Americanized in spite of themselves, in the mode prescribed by their friends and benefactors." But however often and however deeply they offended one another, the two groups felt utterly bound by their Jewishness.

Urban Life

Unlike their German predecessors, who had spread west all the way to California, the eastern European migrants crowded together in the slums of major eastern and midwestern cities: Chicago, Philadelphia, Cleveland, St. Louis, Baltimore, Boston, and of course, New York. By 1910 there were more than half a million Jews squeezed into a 1½-square-mile patch on New York's Lower East Side. Conditions in the slums were deplorable: filthy, smelly, and above all, overcrowded. The apartments were cramped and dark. One contemporary report described a typical tenement flat:

> The parents occupy a small bedroom together with two, three or even four of the younger children. In the kitchen, on cots and on the floor, are the older children; in the front room two or more (in rare cases as many as five) lodgers sleep on the lounge, on the floor, and on cots, and in the fourth bedroom two lodgers . . .

Working conditions were even more appalling. Some of the new immigrants followed the example of the German Jews and became peddlers, lugging their packs door-to-door to earn a few pennies and a lot of derision. (The Jewish peddler seems to have been a favorite target of Irish-American boys with ripe fruit.) Most of the new arrivals became fodder for the growing garment industry, centered at the time in squalid tenement quarters that came to be called "sweatshops." Many immigrants found jobs in the sweatshops because they had gained experience as tailors in the old country. Those unable to sew were hired as unskilled workers, operating the new machinery used

increasingly in the business. Immigrants also favored the clothing industry because it was owned, in large part, by other Jews. Eastern Europeans with memories of pogroms fresh in their minds welcomed the prospect of Jewish bosses, who at least shared their religion.

But a common heritage did not prevent bosses from mistreating sweatshop workers. Laborers earned next to nothing, and as a sympathetic observer sarcastically reported: "They work no longer than to nine o'clock at night, from daybreak." Hot, grimy, and crowded, the shops pushed exhausted workers to the limits of human tolerance, but a majority of immigrants felt they had to accept work on whatever terms it was offered. Garment

Jews do garment work in a New York City tenement in 1889.

work was cyclical, and during the "slow season" jobs were scarce and competition for them fierce.

Like all immigrants, Jews scrimped, saved, and dreamed of a better life. A Chicago inspector reported:

> A very large number speculate on the notion of opening, in course of time, a shop for themselves or going into business of some kind, or educating themselves out of the condition of the working classes. A large part of the tolerance of low wages, long hours of work, and unsanitary condition of the shops, that is, of the tragedy of economic servitude, of poverty, and of suffering, is to be ascribed to this state of mind.

The immigrants did not hope in vain. Within a few generations, many of their descendants would be living in comfort they themselves could scarcely imagine. Although some regarded American materialism as a spiritual trap, most immigrants struggled to better their plight. Grueling hours at work never deterred them from educating themselves in the ways, and especially the language, of the new country. An 1898 report in the *Atlantic Monthly* noted:

> Surely nothing can be more inspiring to the public-spirited citizen, nothing worthier of the interest of the student of immigration, than the sight of a gray-haired tailor, a patriarch in appearance, coming, after a hard day's work at a sweat-shop, to spell "cat, mat, rat," and to grapple with the difficulties of "th" and "w."

Immigrants in urban slums experienced every imaginable discomfort—hunger, sleeplessness, illness, and stifling quarters—but tried not to let these hardships wear at the fabric of domestic life. For generations, shtetl families had clung together through thick and thin, finding stability in well-defined roles. Jewish custom dictated that women reigned over the household and men supervised religious duties and wage earning. In the New World, the sexes divided labor in much the same fashion: Daughters might work in the sweatshops alongside sons until the demands of married life summoned them back to the home, where they sometimes labored at paid needlework to help support the family. Household activity often revolved around the kitchen. By day it harbored the cooking and washing, and by night it turned into a parlor, thus saving families the expense of heating the other rooms.

New Communities

Because New World Jewish society no longer revolved around shtetl life, immigrants had to improvise new communities. One organization important to them was the *landsmanshaft*, a club whose members came from the same shtetl or city in the old country. Most of the landsmanshaft formed between 1903 and 1909; at the height of their popularity, several thousand existed in America's cities, especially New York. Besides giving alienated immigrants a sense of belonging, these societies performed useful services: making burial arrangements and providing insurance, illness benefits, and low-cost loans. Landsmanshaft from the same area— Poland, Romania, or Galicia—might band together to support large charitable projects, such as hospitals or old-age homes. But the clubs were primarily social. The era of the landsmanshaft was short-lived (though by 1938 they still claimed three-quarters of a million members across the country); the members' native-born children, at home in America, rarely required the kind of support furnished by the clubs.

The landsmanshaft were not the only organizations formed by Jews in America to help Jews. Perhaps no other ethnic group supported a greater number or variety of philanthropic activities. As a community, Jewish immigrants placed a high value on helping other Jews, on the tradition of learning, and on the virtue of *tzedokah* (charity). Jews founded hospitals, orphanages, settlement houses (institutions that provided community services, especially in poor urban neighborhoods), Hebrew schools, institutions of higher Jewish learning, and Young Men's and Young Women's Hebrew Associations (the Jewish equivalent of the YMCA and YWCA). One of the most active organizations was the United Hebrew Charities of New York, founded in 1881, which coordinated the efforts of various charitable agencies that helped Jewish immigrants find jobs and places to live.

Jews also found companionship and comfort at the *shul*, the Orthodox synagogue. The German immigrants' brand of Judaism, Reform, had never appealed to the eastern European immigrants. For them traditional Orthodoxy supplied more than a mode of worship, it gave them a way of life, detailing rules and regulations for every imaginable circumstance. Not sur-

prisingly, as the shtetl gave way to the big-city slum, the shtetl religion, Orthodox Judaism, became harder to practice. For example, Orthodox Jews consider Sabbath observance a sacred duty, but sometimes when the Sabbath arrived, they found it impossible to sacrifice a day's wages, particularly when their children were hungry. Such dilemmas began to undermine their religious practices.

Religious custom changed most drastically perhaps for those New World Jews who adopted Reform Judaism. A response to the strictness of Orthodoxy, the Reform movement began in the early 19th century and

Jewish settlers in Montana pose with their rabbi, Samuel Schulman (third from left, bottom row), in a photograph taken ca. 1890.

was transplanted to the American Midwest by German Jews, beginning in the 1840s. The leading reformer of this era, Isaac Mayer Wise (1819–1900), founded Hebrew Union College in Cincinnati, the city where he served as a rabbi for 35 years. Also an author, Wise wrote novels, plays, essays, memoirs, and perhaps most important, a revised prayer book, which included an English or German translation of the Hebrew on each facing page. Through this book, *Minhag America* (*The American Rite*), English was introduced in the services.

The Reform cause Wise championed soon spread, catching on because it allowed for easier accommodation of new scientific ideas (including Darwin's theories of evolution) and for a revision of Jewish theology and ritual more in tune with life in America. Some outward restrictions in Jewish law were relaxed, for instance dietary laws that proved impractical in a frontier setting. The reform movement did not immediately find favor among newer immigrants, especially those from eastern Europe, but in Wise's opinion reform would come as the nation progressed. Followers of American Reform Judaism succeeded in maintaining most of their Old World beliefs and also in bringing those ancient beliefs in line with the evolving ideas of a growing country. Two innovations particularly applauded by Wise were the use of family pews in the synagogue (previously, members had been segregated by sex) and the inclusion of women in the choir.

As the observance of religion changed, so, too, did the role of the religious leader, the rabbi. Traditionally, the shtetl rabbi acted as a combination of teacher, community leader, and judge. In the United States, the power of this traditional figure of authority diminished greatly because law was interpreted by civil courts. In fact, rabbis in the United States relinquished all their customary duties but one: conducting religious services. This loss of status accompanied a general shifting of values within the Jewish community in the New World. Shul attendance dropped dramatically. Still, thousands who lost the habit of everyday religious observance re-

(continued on page 73)

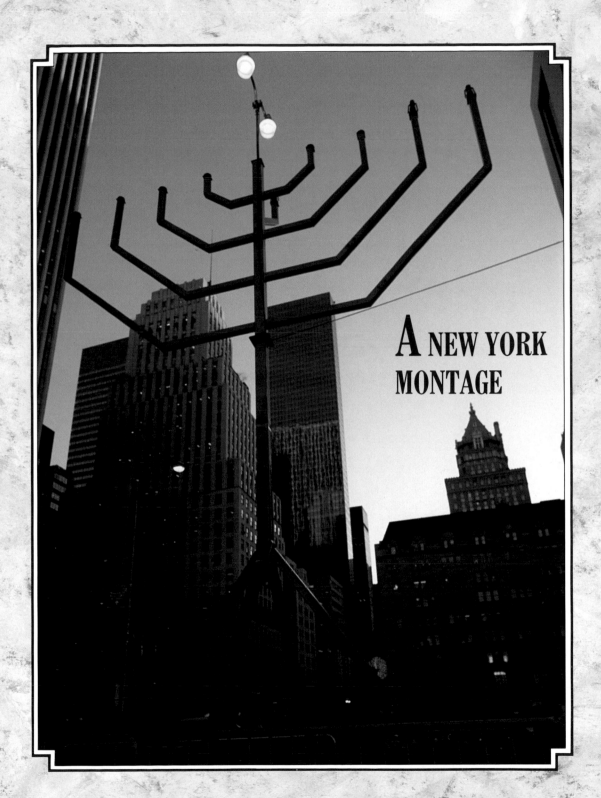

A NEW YORK MONTAGE

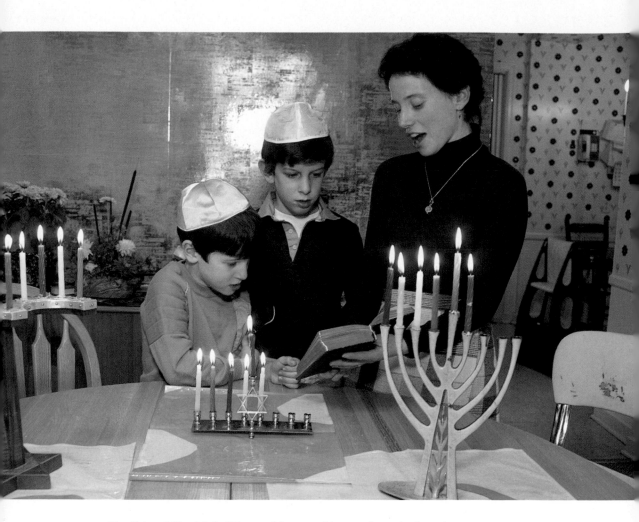

Traditional Jewish holidays celebrate a history of survival against overwhelming odds. The Hanukkah menorah (above)—a nine-branched candelabra lit during the Festival of Lights—symbolizes an oil lamp that held enough fuel for a single night but miraculously burned for eight. At the Passover seder (right), Jews read from the Haggadah, which describes their ancestors' exodus from Egypt in the 13th century B.C.

Modern Judaism divides into three distinct categories. At Orthodox synagogues (above, left) women must gather separately behind a screen to read from the Torah, whereas Reform Judaism—born in the 19th century— allows men and women to worship together and includes innovations such as the confirmation ceremony (below, left). Conservative Judaism—a compromise between the old and the new—now accepts women into the rabbinate. Above, two rabbinical students at the Jewish Theological Seminary meet with their chancellor.

A third of America's 6 million Jews live in New York, where their culture remains a vital force: A Brooklyn pizzeria offers kosher fare; a parade up Manhattan's Fifth Avenue honors the nation of Israel; and couples dance in the Catskills, a mountain resort area long favored by Jewish Americans.

The world of finance includes many venerable firms founded by Jewish Americans. Top executives convene for an informal photo session at Lehman Brothers, a leading Wall Street brokerage that in 1984 merged with Shearson Hayden, Stone Inc. to form Shearson Lehman Brothers, now a subsidiary of American Express.

Editor Abraham Cahan advocated socialism in the pages of his newspaper, the Jewish Daily Forward.

(continued from page 64)

mained believers, and on the High Holy Days—Rosh Hashanah and Yom Kippur—Jews continued to fill the Orthodox shuls. These places of worship exerted a nostalgic, emotional pull. They were links to the old country, and they seemed much warmer and more welcoming than their cosmopolitan stepchild, Reform temples.

The Jewish Press

Some Jewish interests fell by the wayside in America, but others found new life. Few other immigrant groups have taken to journalism as eagerly as the Jews, who enthusias-

Addie Kahn (née Wolff), wife of banker Otto Kahn, epitomized the gentility of New York's German-Jewish elite.

tically published, wrote for, and read newspapers. By 1823, Jewish Americans had their own newspaper; it was called the *Jew* and was published in New York City. Although the *Jew* lasted for only two years, it had many successors. In the second half of the 19th century, the Jewish press bloomed in the United States, producing as many as 90 journals, including the *Israelite* in Cincinnati, the *Jewish Voice* in St. Louis, the *Jewish Spectator* in Memphis, and the *Occident* in Chicago. In addition, Philadelphia, Cleveland, and Montreal all had their own Jewish dailies. Hundreds more of these papers appeared between 1900 and 1920, publishing news and feature articles as well as poetry and fiction by leading Yiddish writers.

The foremost Orthodox paper, the *Yiddisher Tageblatt*, defended traditional religious values, but like all the New York Yiddish newspapers it was pro-labor and democratically oriented. Another paper, the *Tog*, reflected a moderately Zionist viewpoint. The most popular of the Yiddish dailies was the *Jewish Daily Forward*, which at its peak had 200,000 regular readers. Its editor, Abraham Cahan, became one of the most influential people in the immigrant community. A Lithuanian Jew, he came to America in 1882 at the age of 22 and soon gained a reputation as a lively speaker who promoted socialism and the labor movement. Cahan also achieved renown as a writer gifted in both English and Yiddish; his 1917 novel *The Rise of David Levinsky* remains a classic of immigrant life.

But it was as editor of the *Forward* that Cahan wielded the most influence. He strongly believed that socialism was the best form of social and economic organization and that the best way to bring socialism to a wide audience was through a popular newspaper. The *Forward* ran plenty of news and serious commentary, but it also packed in scandal, crime, and human-interest stories. Its most popular feature was an advice column called "A Bintel Brief" ("A Bundle of Letters"), which was a kind of Yiddish "Dear Abby."

The *Forward* supported the Jewish labor unions and contributed generously to strike funds and other pro-labor causes. But it was more than a socialist paper; it was a Jewish paper—the largest Yiddish daily in the world— that offered not only political but practical advice. The *Forward* linked the immigrant community to mysterious America—for example, by explaining the ins and outs of baseball or by insisting, over and over, on the importance of learning English. Cahan was an assimilationist who believed that immigrants needed to become part of the mainstream of society in their new home. He sought to Americanize them, to teach them what they needed to know in order to become Americans. Like later Jewish labor leaders such as Samuel Gompers and David Dubinsky, Cahan believed that immigrant workers could and should work within the system. He died in 1951, but the *Forward* is still being published.

Bankers and Financiers

In the last third of the 19th century and the early years of the 20th, the American economy grew enormously, and workers and owners from many nations participated in the industrial and financial boom. Jewish Americans played a major role in this growth, chiefly through the big New York merchant banks they had founded or built. At first, most of these businessmen were German by birth—Seligman, Loeb, Kuhn, Warburg, Schiff, Guggenheim—but as the 20th century wore on, Jews from eastern Europe also entered what the Germans had once called "our crowd." The Jewish "crowd" arose because a man such as Jacob Schiff, who acted as J. P. Morgan's banker in some of that magnate's early railroad deals, was excluded from the social world inhabited by his client.

Today, many of Wall Street's biggest brokerages and investment banks still bear the names of Jewish-American founders: Shearson Lehman Brothers, Salomon Brothers, Goldman Sachs & Co. These firms are staffed by descendants of the early millionaires and also by the sons and daughters of poor immigrants who made good in subsequent generations. The early banking fortunes have benefited the public as well, with funding for museums, hospitals, schools, and dozens of other foundations and charities.

Bankers were not the only successful Jews who used their fortunes to benefit the general public. Over the years, many Jewish businesspeople have supported philanthropic and cultural causes. Helena Rubenstein (1870–1965), a Polish Jew who came to the United States from Europe at the outbreak of World War I, built her skin-care business into one of the world's largest cosmetics companies. She donated money to many museums, colleges, and organizations that aided needy women and children. In 1953 she established the Helena Rubenstein Foundation to coordinate her philanthropic projects. The Guggenheim family also contributed large sums to education and the arts. Daniel, Simon, and

Solomon Guggenheim were sons of Meyer Guggenheim, a Swiss Jew who immigrated to the United States in 1847 and made a fortune in the business of smelting metallic ores. Daniel Guggenheim and his wife, Florence, established a foundation that sponsors scientific, musical, charitable, medical, and educational projects in the United States and abroad. Simon Guggenheim set up a foundation that awards fellowships (grants of money) to scholars and artists. Solomon Guggenheim, who had amassed a large collection of paintings by modern artists, hired American architect Frank Lloyd Wright to build the Guggenheim Museum in New York City to house the collection and make it available to the public. ∾

JEWISH CULTURE, AMERICAN CULTURE

Jews have played an enormous role in shaping 20th-century American culture through their contributions to theater, literature, painting, sports, and popular entertainment. But the first flowering of Jewish culture in America—the literature of the eastern European immigrants—remained inaccessible to the mainstream of American society for years because it was written in Yiddish, not English.

The earliest Jewish-American writers reached their public through the Yiddish newspapers, which published the work of fine poets. Some of these poets were members of the "Sweatshop School"; their work described the hardships of life in New York City's garment factories. One of the most memorable poems in this tradition, "Meine Yingele" ("My Little Boy"), tells of a father's sadness at leaving for work at dawn and returning home after dark, never seeing his child awake. Later Yiddish poets adopted modern techniques but failed to find an audience among the more sophisticated Jewish Americans whose first language was English, not Yiddish. As the use of Yiddish declined in America, the work of these poets faded from view.

Not all Yiddish literature vanished without a trace, however. Some Yiddish writers produced fiction that earned a wider following on both sides of the Atlantic; later, when these works were translated, they became popular with a still more diverse audience. By the late 19th century, European-Yiddish literature could claim some major novelists, some of whom lived in the United States.

Yiddish Fiction

When he arrived at Ellis Island at the beginning of the 20th century, Sholom Aleichem was known as the outstanding Yiddish writer of his day. His novels, plays, and stories had alerted readers to the literary merits of Yiddish. In America, some of his short stories immediately found a home in New York City's Yiddish newspapers. Aleichem's wry tales, set in the shtetls of Russia, describe the lives of downtrodden Jews, including Tevye the Dairyman, who decades later captivated Broadway audiences as the main character of the musical *Fiddler on the Roof.*

Even greater popularity greeted two later Yiddish novelists, the brothers Israel Joshua and Isaac Bashevis Singer. They were born in Poland, sons of a rabbi, and at an early age were introduced to Jewish scholarship and folklore. I. J. Singer's stories attracted the attention of Abraham Cahan, publisher of the *Jewish Daily Forward,* who hired Singer to serve as the paper's Polish correspondent. Singer emigrated to New York in 1934 and there completed his masterpiece, *The Brothers Ashkenazi,* a massive family chronicle that in translation became popular with American readers.

His younger brother, Isaac Bashevis Singer, observed life in urban Warsaw and in the homely shtetl where his grandfather lived. Urged by his parents to become a rabbi, I. B. Singer instead dedicated himself to writing fiction. At first he wrote in Hebrew, but later he switched to his native tongue, Yiddish. Singer immigrated to the United States in 1935 and, like his brother, began contributing to the *Jewish Daily Forward.* His fic-

Isaac Bashevis Singer has written folktales for children as well as novels for adults.

tion combined realism and folklore to explore the Jews' sadness at the decline of their traditional culture. Singer was introduced to a large American audience through translations of stories such as "Gimpel the Fool" and novels such as *Satan in Goray* and *The Family Moskat.* In 1978, I. B. Singer became the first Yiddish writer to receive the Nobel Prize for literature.

Early Jewish Theater

Jewish culture includes no formal theatrical tradition apart from the comic playlets that annually commemmorate Purim, the holiday celebrating the deliverance of ancient Jews from a massacre by the Persians. Yet dra-

New York's Grand Theatre featured Yiddish stage-idol Jacob Adler in a 1903 production of In the Broken Hearts.

matic theater, more than any other art form, captured the collective imagination of America's early Jewish immigrants. Written and performed in Yiddish, colorful and emotional plays reflected the daily passions of immigrant life.

In the late 19th century, Yiddish performing troupes started appearing on both sides of the Atlantic. New York's first Yiddish production was staged in 1882. Theaters cropped up wherever an audience of Jews could be assembled. The earliest plays—a hodgepodge of historical themes, farce, music, melodrama, and local jokes—poured from the pens of writers who feverishly recycled ancient material. A playwright who needed a high-flown speech might steal it from Shakespeare; a dramatist might simply wrench a masterpiece of world drama into a Jewish setting. (An audience at a Yiddish *Hamlet* was so impressed that it called for the author to take a bow.) These plays used spectacle and emotion to stir the audience, but their success was assured if they focused on two themes: Jewish suffering and Jewish endurance.

Yiddish theater lacked brilliant playwrights, but it teemed with marvelous actors who engaged the hearts of their audiences. At a performance of *The Jewish King Lear*, one man was so distraught by the spectacle of Lear's daughters' ingratitude that he rushed up to the stage shouting, "To hell with your stingy daughter! She has a stone, not a heart!" Gradually the Yiddish theater acquired more sophistication, yet it never won a place among the great theatrical traditions of the West. Like Yiddish poetry and fiction, Yiddish drama reached its maturity in the same moment that its parent culture faded. American Jews adopted English as their native tongue, often shunning Yiddish, and in Europe the Nazi Holocaust wiped out most of the Jewish population. After the 1940s no Yiddish-speaking audience existed. Yet the influence of the great Yiddish actors was not altogether lost. Stella Adler (1901–1992), an American actress, director, and teacher of acting who inspired several generations of actors, was the daughter of Jacob and Sarah Adler, Russian Jewish immigrants who were stars of the Yiddish theater. All six of Jacob and Sarah Adler's children became actors, but Stella Adler had the widest influence on American theater because of her role as a teacher.

The Age of Vaudeville

Jewish-American performers carried their art beyond the immigrant community. The flowering of Yiddish theater coincided with the great age of American vaudeville, a type of music-hall entertainment that featured comedy and singing. Many Jewish-American performers became well-known vaudevillians. Fanny Brice, one

Jewish-American comedienne Fanny Brice (right) starred with actress Judy Garland in the 1937 motion picture Everybody Sing.

In 1936, Al Jolson (in "blackface," holding hat) starred with big-band leader Cab Calloway in the Warner Brothers musical The Singing Kid.

of the leading Jewish comics of her era, delighted audiences of all ethnic backgrounds with Yiddish-accent stories about immigrant culture. People flocked to see her at the Ziegfeld Follies—the spectacular revue put together by Jewish impresario Florenz Ziegfeld. (Decades later, Barbra Streisand, another Jewish star, portrayed Fanny on the stage and then on the screen in the musical *Funny Girl*.)

The vaudeville era (1880–1930) produced a host of Jewish comics, singers, and dancers, including Eddie Cantor, George Burns, and Jack Benny. The Marx Brothers originated their comic style on the vaudeville stage and then transferred it to movies with such hits as *Duck Soup* (1933) and *A Night at the Opera* (1935), lampoons of high society.

Jewish-American comedy flourished also in the stand-up routines of Henny Youngman and Myron Cohen and in the daring monologues of Lenny Bruce. Some Jewish-American performers—such as Sid Caesar, Joan Rivers, and Buddy Hackett—had great success on television. Many of these later comedians started out performing in the "Borscht Belt," the string of Jewish resorts in New York's Catskill Mountains. Mel Brooks and Woody Allen, who got their start in these resorts, went on to stellar careers in the movies. Another Borscht Belt star, Jackie Mason, brought his comic routines to Broadway, delighting Jews and non-Jews alike.

Composers and Musicians

Jewish Americans have contributed greatly to Broadway musicals and to the nation's storehouse of popular tunes. In the early 1900s, before technology could adequately reproduce sound, families created their own music at home on the parlor piano. Many of these tunes came from the music publishers clustered on New York City's

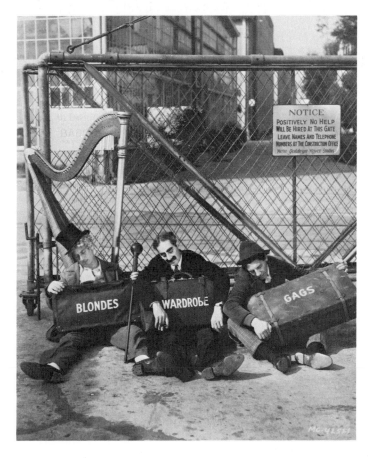

A publicity photo taken during the 1930s on the Metro-Goldwyn-Mayer lot features three of the four Marx Brothers (from left): Harpo, Groucho, and Chico.

28th Street, known as "Tin Pan Alley" because some of the songs cranked out there had all the grace of clattering cookware. In the first quarter of the 20th century, Tin Pan Alley published the works of many Jewish-American composers, including such popular favorites as "Waltz Me Around Again, Willy" and "Those Wedding Bells Shall Not Ring Out." The Alley also served as a training ground for talented young musicians.

One of America's leading composers got his start in Tin Pan Alley. George Gershwin (born Jakob Bruskin Gershvin) was barely 20 years old when he wrote his first hit, "Swanee." Within a few years, his jazz-flavored compositions were featured in Broadway musicals. Together with his brother, Ira, a lyricist, Gershwin wrote songs—including "I Got Rhythm" and "Love Is Here to Stay"—that were performed by such popular singers as Billie Holliday, Ella Fitzgerald, and Frank Sinatra. Gersh-

In May 1982, pianist Vladimir Horowitz practiced in preparation for his first English recital in 30 years.

win's true genius, however, was revealed in the concert hall. His symphonic compositions, especially *Rhapsody in Blue* and *An American in Paris*, brought new respectability to jazz, a purely American art form. Gershwin's 1935 opera *Porgy and Bess*, which contains the hit "Summertime," depicts the lives of poor southern blacks. Gershwin completed the opera, his major work, at the age of 37. Two years later he died of a brain tumor.

Gershwin's contemporary Richard Rodgers also brought innovations to musical theater. Teamed with lyricists Lorenz Hart and Oscar Hammerstein II, Rodgers produced some of the most successful shows in Broadway history, including *Oklahoma!* (1943), which incorporated themes of American folk music, a daring experiment for its time. Another great Jewish-American songwriter of the early 20th century was Irving Berlin, who wrote "God Bless America" and "White Christmas."

In the area of classical music, Jewish-American composers and performers have added richly to the nation's musical heritage. Leonard Bernstein, the son of Russian Jewish immigrants, excelled as a conductor, composer, and pianist. At the age of 40 he was appointed director of the New York Philharmonic—the first American-born musician to hold that position with a major U.S. orchestra. Soon Bernstein began to compose music as well as conduct it. His ballet *Fancy Free* was later expanded into the hit musical *On the Town*. His Broadway musical *West Side Story* (1957), an updating of Shakespeare's *Romeo and Juliet*, became a movie that won four Academy Awards in 1961.

Another influential composer of Russian-Jewish descent was Aaron Copland (1900–1990), who studied music in Paris and then became a leader among contemporary American composers, combining musical themes from folk music and jazz with the spare, abstract style of modern music. In 1945 his ballet *Appalachian Spring* won the Pulitzer Prize for music; he also produced concert-hall pieces, including piano sonatas, symphonies, and an opera (*The Tender Land*, 1954). Copland was a member of many honorary societies, including the National Institute of Arts and Letters in New York and the Royal Academy of Music in London.

Jewish Americans have also excelled as performers of classical music. Among these outstanding performers are pianists Vladimir Horowitz, Rudolf Serkin, and Gary Graffman; violinists Jascha Heifetz, Yehudi Menuhin, Itzhak Perlman, and Isaac Stern; cellist Leonard Rose; and opera singers Robert Merrill, Roberta Peters, and Beverly Sills.

Arthur Rubinstein (1887–1982), a Polish-born Jew who became a U.S. citizen in 1946, is regarded by many as the foremost classical pianist of the 20th century. Practicing six to nine hours a day, he honed his technique into a virtuosity that won him international acclaim. Rubinstein made more than 200 recordings of the piano compositions of Beethoven, Mozart, Chopin, and other composers. He was awarded the U.S. Medal of Freedom in 1976.

One of the most remarkable Jewish musicians of recent times was Canadian pianist and composer Glenn Gould (1932–1982), who earned a worldwide reputation as an innovative interpreter of the works of 18th-century composer Johann Sebastian Bach. Beginning in the 1950s, Gould also composed his own works. He gave up his concert career in the mid-1960s and devoted the rest of his life to recording in the studio. Just months before his death he rounded out his career by recording Bach's *Goldberg Variations*, a complex piece that he had first recorded 30 years earlier.

Jewish performers have also contributed to the field of popular music. Benny Goodman (1909–1986) was a clarinetist and orchestra leader who in the 1930s became known as the "King of Swing" for his fast, rhythmical jazz. His orchestra was one of the most popular swing bands in the country; he also led smaller groups, trios and quartets, that introduced jazz to white audiences. Goodman hired black musicians, becoming the first white orchestra leader to present racially mixed popular jazz groups. In 1962 he took a jazz band to the Soviet Union on a U.S. State Department tour. He also played classical clarinet with several symphony orchestras.

Contemporary Jewish folk and rock music stars include Paul Simon and Art Garfunkel, Carole King, Phil Ochs, and Robert Zimmerman—better known as singer-songwriter Bob Dylan. A native of Minnesota, Dylan went to New York in 1960 to begin a career as a folksinger. He soon emerged as a songwriter whose lyrics challenged social injustice. "Blowin' In the Wind," perhaps his most enduring hit, became an anthem of the civil rights movement, while "The Times They Are A-Changin' " heralded the era of student protest. Dylan's later career has been characterized by many changes in style and subject matter. In the late 1970s he announced his conversion to Christianity.

Hollywood

Jewish Americans have enriched nearly every realm of American culture, but none more so than film. One of the most popular entertainers of the early 20th century was singer Al Jolson, a veteran of circuses, vaudeville, and Broadway. In 1927, Jolson made cinema history with his performance in the autobiographical film *The Jazz Singer*, the first feature-length "talkie." Jolson's singing thrilled moviegoers who were used to silent films and forced Hollywood's major studios to switch to sound movies.

Jews formed and ran all but one of Hollywood's production companies in the 1920s and 1930s. The Goldwyn and Mayer of Metro-Goldwyn-Mayer, the Fox of 20th Century–Fox, the Warner Brothers, and Paramount's chief, Adolph Zukor, were all of Jewish descent. Most were born in poverty in eastern Europe and came to the United States when they were young, drifting into various jobs before discovering that a fortune could be made in "nickelodeons," America's first movie theaters. These primitive cinemas consisted of rented storefronts with rows of wooden chairs on which audiences sat for hours, entranced by silent films. Later, operators built

In 1962, Bob Dylan released his first album, Bob Dylan, *a collection that included many traditional folk songs.*

larger theaters, until eventually movie houses became lavish, palatial structures. The entrepreneurs who operated the movie houses moved into the distribution and production of films. By the 1920s, motion pictures were a million-dollar industry presided over by immigrants.

The studio owners, with their miserable educations, Yiddish accents, and unabashed love of money, molded America's popular taste more than any other force in the 20th century. The Hollywood moguls ran their studios with an iron fist, controlling every detail of every film, with a brilliant understanding of the fantasies that touched the imagination of a huge and diverse nation.

Two memorable moguls were Irving Grant Thalberg and David Oliver Selznick. Thalberg left Brooklyn for Hollywood while still a teenager and found work at Universal Studios. At 25 he became production manager of Metro-Goldwyn-Mayer and steered the studio toward quality films based on literary classics or best-sellers. His successes included *Grand Hotel* (1932), *Mutiny on the Bounty* (1935), and *Romeo and Juliet* (1936). Thalberg inspired novelist F. Scott Fitzgerald to create a similar character, Monroe Stahr, in *The Last Tycoon*, an unfinished novel set in Hollywood.

Selznick was the son of motion-picture producer Lewis Selznick. The younger Selznick worked for a number of studios before founding his own company. He produced such hits as *Gone With the Wind* (1933), *Anna Karenina* (1935), *Tom Sawyer* (1937), and *A Farewell to Arms* (1943), all based on literary classics.

Thalberg, Selznick, and the other moguls seldom hid their Jewish roots, yet they painstakingly suppressed all traces of Jewishness in their movies. Many successful Jewish-American directors, screenwriters, and actors also downplayed their Jewish identity for fear that Jews would not become popular with non-Jewish audiences. Well-known and successful Jewish actors include Lauren Bacall, James Caan, Tony Curtis, Kirk Douglas, Richard Dreyfuss, Peter Falk, Elliot Gould, Goldie Hawn, Dustin Hoffman, Madeline Kahn, Danny Kaye, Jerry Lewis, Walter Matthau, Bette Midler, Paul Muni,

Hollywood mogul Louis B. Mayer shows visitors the set of Ben Hur, *about 1925.*

Paul Newman, Edward G. Robinson, Rod Steiger, Gene Wilder, and Shelley Winters. Hollywood also boasts some famous converts to Judaism, including Marilyn Monroe, Elizabeth Taylor, and Sammy Davis, Jr.

Many of these stars worked under the guidance of Jewish directors such as Josef von Sternberg, Erich von Stroheim, Ernst Lubitch, George Cukor, Sidney Lumet, Paul Mazursky, and Mike Nichols. Their European colleagues Fritz Lang, Otto Preminger, and Billy Wilder came to the United States during World War II to escape from the Nazis, as did some of Hollywood's greatest composers and camera operators.

One of Hollywood's most successful and influential contemporary figures is Steven Spielberg, born in 1947. As both a director and a producer, Spielberg has thrilled audiences with a series of adventure movies noted for their pulse-pounding excitement and outstanding special effects: *Jaws, Close Encounters of the Third Kind, Raiders of the Lost Ark, E.T.: The Extraterrestrial,* and *Jurassic Park.* He has also produced thoughtful films about oppression and racism: *The Color Purple* and the Academy-Award-winning *Schindler's List,* which deals with the Nazi Holocaust.

In 1987 acclaimed filmmaker Steven Spielberg accepted a special Oscar, the Irving Thalberg Memorial Award, for his outstanding achievements in motion pictures.

One star who has used his Jewish-American identity in his work is Woody Allen, a stand-up comedian and writer who became a noted film actor, writer, and director. In 1978, Allen won Academy awards for best screenplay, best direction, and best movie for his film *Annie Hall*. In 1987 he again earned an Oscar, this time for his screenplay for *Hannah and Her Sisters*. Allen's humor often draws upon the anxieties, obsessions, and preoccupations of intellectual city-dwellers—themes rooted in his experience as a New York Jew but nevertheless interesting to a wide audience both in the United States and abroad.

Jewish Fiction

Most early Jewish-American literary works were straightforward depictions of the immigrant experience, such as Cahan's *The Rise of David Levinsky* (1917). Later novels, such as Daniel Fuchs's *Williamsburg Trilogy* (1934–37) and Henry Roth's *Call It Sleep* (1939), probed more deeply into the Jewish-American mind. Their contemporary Nathanael West did not deal with specifically Jewish themes, but his masterpiece, *Miss Lonelyhearts* (1933) captured the anxiety of America during the Depression and of characters ruled by false hopes and unrealized dreams.

The next generation of Jewish-American writers tried to explore their people's experience not only by using plots, characters, and themes of Jewish life but also by creating a new style that echoed the rhythms of immigrant English and restored to American fiction the vitality of the spoken word. Canadian-born novelist Saul Bellow deserves the greatest credit for this innovation. The son of Russian Jews, Bellow moved to Chicago in 1923 at the age of eight. He grew up surrounded by a mixture of Yiddish and Chicagoese that he forged into a style shaped by great learning and intelligence. One critic called Bellow's writing "the first major new style in American prose since those of Hemingway and Faulkner: a mingling of high-flown intellectual bravado with racy-tough street Jewishness." In Bellow's 1953 novel *The Adventures of Augie Marsh*, the narrator describes Chicago with both humor and anguish:

> Around was Chicago. In its repetition it exhausted your imagination of details and units, more units than the cells of the brain and bricks of Babel. . . . A mysterious tremor, dust, vapor, emanation of stupendous effort traveled with the air, over me . . . and over the clinics, clinks, factories, flophouses, morgue, skid row. As before the work of Egypt and Assyria, as before a sea, you're nothing here. Nothing.

Bellow's other novels include *Seize the Day, Herzog,* and

Cynthia Ozick's novel The Messiah of Stockholm *met with great critical acclaim when it was published in 1987.*

Followers surround poet Alan Ginsberg as he chants a mantra in London's Hyde Park in 1967.

Humboldt's Gift. In 1976 he won the Nobel Prize for literature.

Brooklyn-born Bernard Malamud, the son of Russian Jewish immigrants, wrote gripping narratives that hark back to the tradition of Yiddish folk stories and dignify the common man. His first novel, *The Natural* (1952), is about a baseball hero with miraculous powers. *The Assistant* (1957) describes the relationship between an old Jewish grocer and a young hoodlum. *The Fixer* (1966), which is set in czarist Russia and tells of a Jewish handyman wrongly imprisoned for the murder of a Christian boy, won the Pulitzer Prize for literature. Malamud also wrote brilliant short stories that appeared in several volumes, including *The Magic Barrel* (1958) and *Rembrandt's Hat* (1973). A collected edition of his short fiction was published in 1983, three years before his death.

Philip Roth, a novelist born in Newark, New Jersey, has burlesqued middle-class Jewish culture in novels such as *Goodbye, Columbus* (1960) and *Portnoy's Complaint* (1969). Norman Mailer has gained fame both for fiction *(The Naked and the Dead)* and journalism *(The Executioner's Song)*. J. D. Salinger produced an American classic in his short novel *The Catcher in the Rye*, the moving tale of a teenage boy's anxieties; he also chronicled the lives of the part-Jewish Glass family in *Franny and Zooey*. Cynthia Ozick, one of the most devout of the major Jewish-American writers, has produced collections of short stories *(The Pagan Rabbi)* as well as successful novels *(The Messiah of Stockholm)*.

Jews have also contributed to American poetry. Allen Ginsberg commands perhaps the widest following of contemporary Jewish poets. His most celebrated work, *Howl*, attacks American materialism. Upon its publication in 1956 it became an icon of the avant-garde poets and musicians of the Beat movement. Five years later Ginsberg wrote *Kaddish* (Hebrew for the ancient prayer for the dead), an elegy to his mother, a Russian immigrant who suffered from mental illness.

The Fine Arts

The Old Testament commandment "Thou shalt not make unto thee any graven images, or any likeness of anything" (Exodus, 20:4) echoed through centuries of Jewish culture. With few exceptions, Jews traditionally were not exposed to drawing or painting. That changed in America. In 1889, the Educational Alliance on the Lower East Side of New York, financed by assimilated German Jews, opened its doors to offer courses in various disciplines, including the fine arts, to eastern European immigrants. These classes evolved into the Alliance Art School, a training ground for some of the country's finest Jewish-American artists, including Ben Shahn, Louise Nevelson, Mark Rothko, Adolph Gottlieb, and Barrett Newman.

In New York especially, Jewish Americans helped usher in modern art, introducing it to the public through exhibitions at places such as Gallery 291, operated by a German-Jewish photographer named Alfred Stieglitz. Among the new artists Stieglitz showcased were two East Side immigrants, Max Weber and Abraham Walkowitz, who had studied in Paris. Both influenced the development of 20th-century painters, including fellow New

Ben Shahn painted The Passion of Sacco and Vanzetti *in 1931–32.*

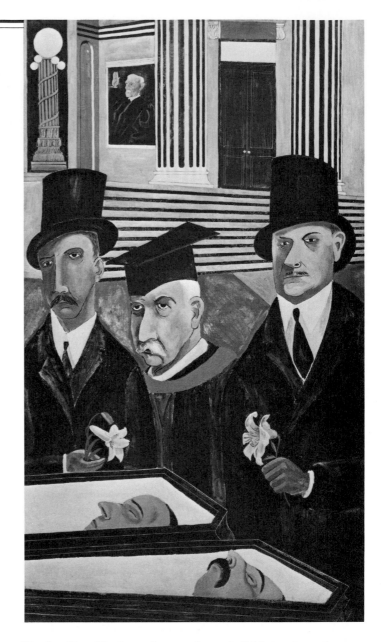

Yorker Ben Shahn, who was born in Lithuania and came to America in 1906. Shahn first gained recognition with a series of works inspired by his dismay at the execution in Massachusetts in 1927 of two Italian immigrants; *The Passion of Sacco and Vanzetti* now hangs in New York's

Whitney Museum. During the 1930s Shahn worked as a government photographer, recording America's rural poverty. He also assisted Mexican painter Diego Rivera in creating murals for Rockefeller Center in New York. Later in his career, Shahn designed stained-glass windows for the Temple Beth Israel in Buffalo, New York.

Louise Nevelson, born in Russia, gained fame as a sculptor in America. She created large, abstract wood sculptures; she also filled wooden forms with found objects to create structures that used everyday items and rubbish in surprising and thought-provoking ways.

Painter Mark Rothko was a leading figure in the "New York School" that dominated the art world in the 1950s.

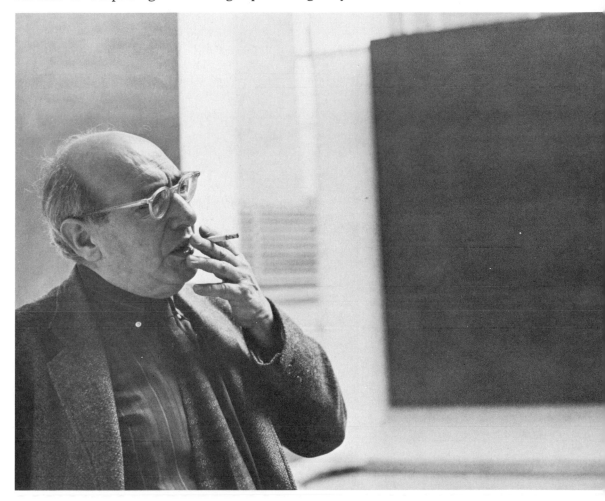

Painter Mark Rothko was also born in Russia. He immigrated to the United States with his parents in 1913, and in 1925 he settled in New York City and dedicated himself to painting. His most characteristic work was a series of immense canvases on which large areas of vibrant, glowing color appear to float in space. Many of his works are in the National Gallery of Art in Washington, D.C.

Sports

Swimmer Mark Spitz won an amazing seven gold medals at the 1972 Olympic Games.

Like music, literature, and the arts, the world of sports has been enriched by the efforts of Jewish Americans. Hank Greenberg (1911–1986) was a power-hitting first baseman for the Detroit Tigers baseball team from 1933 through 1946 (except for the war years, 1941–45).

Greenberg, a member of baseball's Hall of Fame, was the American League's Most Valuable Player in 1935 and 1940.

Another baseball great was Sandy Koufax (b. 1935), a left-handed pitcher for the Brooklyn and L.A. Dodgers from 1955 through 1966. Koufax, also a member of the Hall of Fame, is noted for having pitched four no-hitters. He was the National League's Most Valuable Player in 1963 and won the Cy Young Award, given to baseball's top pitcher, in 1963, 1965, and 1966.

California-born swimmer Mark Spitz (born 1950) set 35 world records in his sport. He began serious training at the age of eight and in 1967 won five gold medals in the American Games, setting five world records in the process. He performed well in the 1968 Olympic Games and thereafter swam for four national championship teams. In 1971 he won the Amateur Athletic Union's trophy for the outstanding amateur athlete of the year. Spitz's greatest performance came in the 1972 Olympic Games, when he set four world records, helped relay teams set three additional records, and won seven gold medals. ➣

In a 1909 demonstration, two young socialists carry banners bearing identical slogans in Yiddish and in English.

EDUCATION AND ADVANCEMENT

For a great many Jewish immigrants and their children, one of the most important aspects of life in America was the opportunity to receive an education. They came from countries where there was little or no public education to a country with a system of public schools and free public libraries that was unique in the world.

Most of the Jewish immigrants, especially the poor Jews, took advantage of America's free educational system to advance themselves intellectually and economically. This theme—the immigrants' thirst for knowledge and their drive to obtain an education—was reflected in many novels about Jewish immigrant life, including Anzia Yezierska's *Bread Givers* (1925). Many Jewish immigrants worked all day and went to night school to learn English or to become American citizens. Leo Rosten's *The Education of Hyman Kaplan* (1937) portrays with affectionate humor the night-school studies of a Jewish immigrant striving to become a U.S. citizen. As a group, Jewish immigrants placed a high value on American citizenship and the opportunity to take part in a representative government; the obligations and privileges of citizenship are still felt by American Jews, who consistently have a higher voting record than the U.S. population at large.

A number of institutions helped Jews achieve their educational goals. Until the second half of the 20th century, the majority of American Jews were concentrated in the New York City area, and the New York Public Library enabled many of them to educate themselves by reading. Many volumes of memoirs and autobiographies by Jewish immigrants and their children tell of long hours spent in the library's reading rooms and of the delight that people felt in having access to books.

New York's public colleges played an enormous role in educating the sons and daughters of the immigrants. These second-generation Jews attended City College, Hunter College, and Brooklyn College, where they acquired the educational qualifications for entering professions such as law, science, and medicine. City College, in particular, numbered among its graduates hundreds of future doctors, lawyers, writers, and scientists, including novelist Bernard Malamud, physician and scientist Jonas Salk, and Supreme Court justice Felix Frankfurter.

The number of Jewish students attending college, and their proportion in the nation's universities, rose steadily. In 1916–1917, there were 14,500 Jewish college students in the United States—about 3 percent of all college students. By 1937, there were 105,000 Jewish students, or slightly more than 9 percent of the total. The number of Jewish students increased despite a painful barrier: Starting in the 1920s, many of the nation's best universities and law and medical schools introduced quotas, systems to limit the number of Jewish students—and also Jewish faculty members—to a mere handful. Not until the late 1950s did these quotas begin to disappear. At that time, young Jews surged into the top schools and, a few years later, into the professions.

In 1964, 80 percent of all young Jews in the United States attended college. The 1960s and 1970s saw a sharp rise in the number of courses in Jewish history and

In 1952 Dr. Jonas Salk produced the first polio vaccine that effectively protected children from the crippling disease.

literature offered by schools and universities; some schools have established whole departments of Jewish studies. Jewish Americans are now very well represented in the nation's universities, both as teachers and as students. By the 1980s, nearly 17 percent of the teaching positions in U.S. colleges and universities were filled by Jews. In 1990, almost 90 percent of American Jews had attended college, and one-third of these had obtained graduate degrees.

Thinkers and Achievers

Many American Jews have been influential as scholars, scientists, activists, and professionals, but few can have had a broader or more significant effect than Abraham Flexner (1866–1959), an educator who was born in Louisville, Kentucky. Flexner taught in a Louisville high school before opening his own school in 1900. He received a M.A. degree from Harvard University in 1906, studied in Berlin, and then went to work as a researcher for the Carnegie Foundation, which assigned him to survey the 144 medical schools then operating in the United States. Flexner's report was both shocking in its criticism of American medical training and brilliant in its suggestions for improvement. The Flexner Report revolutionized American medical training—the nation's worst medical schools were closed and the American Medical Association adopted new guidelines for education. Flexner went on to conduct a similar study of schools of social work and to organize the Institute for Advanced Study in Princeton, New Jersey, which encouraged the immigration of Jewish physicist Albert Einstein into the United States.

Two Jewish-American physicians, Jonas Salk and Albert Sabin, made scientific breakthroughs that changed the lives of millions of children around the world. Salk, who obtained his first medical degree from New York University College of Medicine in 1939, spent years working on vaccines to protect people from common diseases. In 1952 he produced the first vaccine against poliomyelitis, a crippling childhood disease. Five years later a different version of the polio vaccine—one that could be given orally instead of in an injection—was developed by Albert Sabin, who had also studied medicine at New York University. The Sabin vaccine became the form most widely used in the United States and around the world.

Beginning in the 1940s, a group of Jewish-American writers, editors, and critics called the "New York intellectuals" brought new life to American literary and political writing. They taught college classes, wrote books of literary and social criticism, and edited and wrote for some of the country's top journals on public affairs. Among them were Norman Cousins, who edited the *Sat-*

urday Review of Literature, Philip Rahv of the *Partisan Review*, Elliott Cohen and Norman Podhoretz of *Commentary*, and Robert Silvers and Barbara Epstein of the *New York Review of Books*. Most of these journals were liberal and progressive in their orientation. The most political was *Dissent*, whose founder, Irving Howe, was a lifelong believer in democratic socialism. Howe became a leading literary critic and social historian. Among his important works are literary biographies of Sherwood Anderson, William Faulkner, and Thomas Hardy, as well as *World of Our Fathers* (1976), a study of eastern European Jewish immigration to the United States between 1880 and 1924.

Another important figure in New York intellectual circles was Alfred Kazin, author of *On Native Grounds* (1942), a survey of American literature, and three biographical works, *A Walker in the City* (1951), *Starting Out in the Thirties* (1965), and *New York Jew* (1978). Lionel Trilling, who was educated at New York City's Columbia University and taught there from 1931 until his death in 1975, wrote literary biographies of Matthew Arnold and E. M. Forster as well as many essays on social and literary subjects. He interpreted the psychological insights of Sigmund Freud for American readers in *Freud and the Crisis of Our Culture* (1955) and *The Life and Work of Sigmund Freud* (1962).

Although American Jews have often been identified with the literary and intellectual world, they have also been active in the military, in government, and in law. Hyman Rickover (1900–1986) was born in Russia, brought to the United States as a child, and raised in an ethnic neighborhood in Chicago. A diligent student, he built a brilliant academic record that won him admission to the U.S. Naval Academy, after which he went on to a career as a Navy officer. Rickover was convinced that it would be possible to build a nuclear-powered submarine, and after World War II he led the Navy's research into nuclear propulsion. Under his leadership, the first nuclear-powered sub, the *Nautilus*, was launched in 1955. He also participated in the development of nuclear

Alfred Kazin was a respected author and intellectual.

During his 23 years as a Supreme Court justice, Louis Brandeis championed the cause of free speech.

energy plants. A controversial figure who was sometimes criticized for his outspoken opinions, Rickover was promoted to rear admiral in 1953, to vice admiral in 1958, and to full admiral in 1973.

America's Jews have played a role in legal scholarship and in the country's justice system. The first Jew to be appointed to the Supreme Court was Louis D. Brandeis, the son of German Jewish immigrants. Born in Louisville, Kentucky, Brandeis obtained a law degree from Harvard University and set up practice in Boston, frequently working without pay for causes he deemed worthy. He repeatedly took on big business in celebrated courtroom battles and helped to establish maximum working hours and minimum wages for all Americans. President Woodrow Wilson appointed Brandeis to the Supreme Court in 1916—an appointment that caused some controversy, as Brandeis was opposed by both big business interests and anti-Semites within the government. The U.S. Senate approved the appointment, however, after months of heated debate, and Brandeis served on the Supreme Court for 23 years. Brandeis University in Waltham, Massachusetts, named in honor of the jurist, now contains the world's largest collection of documents, books, and other artifacts relating to the history of Jews in America.

Felix Frankfurter, born in Austria, was brought to the United States at the age of 12, knowing no English. Eight years later he graduated third in his class from City College of New York; in 1906 he graduated with highest honors from Harvard Law School. Frankfurter wrote articles supporting liberal and pro-labor causes for the *New Republic* and the *Atlantic Monthly*; he also taught law at Harvard. President Franklin D. Roosevelt appointed him to the Supreme Court in 1939. Throughout his 23 years on the Supreme Court, Frankfurter urged that the court operate with restraint, insisting that its business was to decide cases, not to create a "brave new world," whether liberal or conservative. He believed that government by judges was a poor substitute for government by the people.

In 1993, Ruth Bader Ginsburg became the second woman to serve as a Supreme Court justice. Born in Brooklyn, she attended Cornell University, Harvard Law School, and Columbia Law School and later taught at Rutgers University and at Columbia. She served as the director of the Women's Rights Project of the American Civil Liberties Union during the late 1960s and early 1970s, during which time she argued six landmark cases involving gender discrimination before the Supreme Court (she won five of them, establishing that unequal

In 1993 Ruth Bader Ginsburg became the second female justice on the United States Supreme Court.

treatment of women and men was unconstitutional). In 1980, President Jimmy Carter appointed Ginsburg to the U.S. Court of Appeals, and in 1993, President Bill Clinton named her to the Supreme Court.

Jews and the Labor Movement

Jewish Americans became identified with political activism in the 1880s, when the mass of refugees arrived from eastern Europe. Among these immigrants were some who had witnessed the wave of revolutions that in 1848–

49 swept across Italy, France, Austria, Hungary, Poland, and Germany. Even those born after the ferment subsided shared a memory of its effects. In the United States this memory surfaced in the form of a passionate interest in social reform. Jewish Americans flung themselves into the labor frays that helped define the political life of the United States for many years.

Many of the Jews who landed in America in the 1880s settled in New York City and immediately sought work. Thousands found jobs in the sweatshops, toiling at sewing machines for 12 to 15 hours a day. Employers often required them to work straight through the week, hanging signs that read, "If you don't come in on Sunday, don't come in on Monday."

Immigrants endured this treatment because they had a clear goal: saving enough money to pay for their family's passage from Europe. But the daily grind of the sweatshops became too much even for self-denying immigrants, and some rebelled, blaming their suffering on an economic system that rewarded only competition and financial gain. Those who had been exposed to the

A New York City sweatshop in the early 1900s.

new European political ideology of socialism argued that the workplace would be more humane if businesses were taken from the hands of individual owners and placed under the joint stewardship of labor and management.

Wretched conditions in the sweatshops finally outweighed the security of steady work, and in the 1880s and 1890s laborers organized small work-stoppage strikes. Often they won concessions from employers, although once a walkout ended the strikers tended to settle into the old routine rather than creating a permanent industry-wide union. A core of labor leaders kept the union movement alive, however, and gradually convinced their fellow workers that they must band together if they hoped to gain power. By the end of the 19th century, unions and federations of unions had begun forming in cities across America. In New York, the United Hebrew Trades was organized in 1888; within three years, 40 unions were associated with it. Chicago workers laid the foundation for a labor federation with the Jewish Workers Educational Society; in Philadelphia, it was the Jewish Federation of Labor.

Two of the most important of the early labor leaders were Samuel Gompers of the American Federation of Labor (AFL) and David Dubinsky of the International Ladies Garment Workers Union (ILGWU). Both were Jewish immigrants. Gompers was born in London in 1850 and came to the United States at the age of 13. Soon he had gotten a job and joined the Cigarmakers Union in New York City. Gompers worked his way up through the union ranks until, in 1886, he became the founder and first president of one of the nation's largest labor organizations, the American Federation of Labor. He served as the AFL's president until his death in 1924. Gompers's goals for the AFL included eliminating racial discrimination in the local unions and directing the unions away from political and revolutionary attitudes toward a more practical, economic function. Unlike some earlier union leaders who felt that the unions should advance the cause of socialism or even communism, Gompers favored what he called a "pure and simple" unionism that concentrated its efforts on improving the economic standing of workers within the capitalist system.

The International Ladies Garment Workers Union was formed in 1900. At first it was a cluster of small unions that struggled vainly to win concessions from the clothing manufacturers—some of whom were themselves Jewish immigrants—who employed the thousands of young immigrant women in New York's sweatshops. In 1910 the ILGWU staged a prolonged and bitter strike that ended in a compromise negotiated by Jewish-American lawyer Louis D. Brandeis. The next year a young Polish immigrant named David Dubinsky—who had been arrested several times in Europe for union activity, which was sternly suppressed by most European regimes—arrived in New York. He joined the ILGWU, held a series of offices, and by 1932 had become president of the union. Like Gompers, Dubin-

Two strikers walk the picket line in 1910.

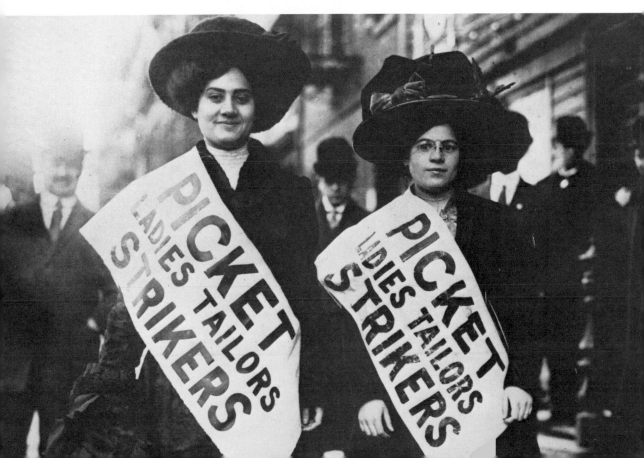

sky believed in the ideals of socialism, but he also believed that the cause of labor could be advanced only within a democratic framework, and that labor unions should operate within the prevailing economic system, not attempt to destroy it. Also like Gompers, Dubinsky was determined to keep the American labor movement from being taken over by communists, who had become increasingly visible in union activity. Both Gompers and Dubinsky helped to quash the communist element within the labor movement and moved the labor unions into the mainstream of American society.

Jewish-American Politics

In the late 19th and early 20th centuries, the German-Jewish community in the United States generally supported the Republican party. A Republican president, Theodore Roosevelt, appointed the first Jewish Cabinet

David Dubinsky, the president of the International Ladies Garment Workers Union, speaks at a rally at Madison Square Garden in 1945.

member: Oscar S. Straus, who served as secretary of commerce and labor. In the 1920s, however, American Jews shifted their loyalties to the Democratic party. In 1928 they rallied behind Democratic presidential candidate Alfred E. Smith, whose campaign manager was Belle Moskowitz, a prominent Jewish-American reformer, and who had spoken out vigorously against the Ku Klux Klan, a racist and anti-Semitic organization. Many Jews also approved of Smith's liberal policies, which called for public health services and pro-labor legislation.

On October 2, 1943, President Franklin D. Roosevelt appointed Judge Samuel I. Rosenman to the White House staff.

Smith was defeated by Herbert Hoover, but in 1932 American Jews supported another Democratic candidate, Franklin D. Roosevelt, who endorsed many of the same policies. Jewish-American support for President Roosevelt remained strong throughout World War II, despite the fact that the U.S. government refused to allow the persecuted Jews of Europe to seek sanctuary in the United States. Nevertheless, Roosevelt was admired by the Jewish-American community not only as America's leader in the war against the Nazis but also as a liberal, progressive president who appointed a number of Jewish Americans to national office.

In the years since Roosevelt's death, most Jews have voted for Democratic candidates. In the presidential elections of the 1960s, a majority of Jews voted for Dem-

Many prominent Jewish Americans joined with Martin Luther King, Jr., on his historic 1965 march between the Alabama cities of Selma and Montgomery.

ocrats John F. Kennedy, Lyndon B. Johnson, and Hubert H. Humphrey. The pattern continued through the 1992 election, in which 78 percent of Jewish voters supported the victorious Democratic candidate, Bill Clinton, compared with 12 percent for Republican George Bush.

In the 1960s, Jewish voting reflected a widespread sympathy for the civil rights movement, which attempted to secure antidiscriminatory legislation and to guarantee voting rights for black Americans. As early as the 1930s Jews had identified with racism directed against black Americans and worked to eliminate it. They helped found the National Association for the Advancement of Colored People (NAACP), which remains one of the leading civil rights organizations in the country. African-American civil rights leader Martin Luther King, Jr., once remarked that "it would be impossible to record the contribution that the Jewish people have made toward the Negro's struggle for freedom—it has been so great."

The causes of Jewish progressivism have long been debated. Some people think that Jews see in liberal social programs a reflection of the ethical and charitable beliefs that are woven into ancient Jewish teachings. Jewish-American scholar and writer Irving Howe suggested that the liberalism of American Jews "was based on at least two factors: the once-powerful tradition of Jewish socialism, now fading but still felt and remembered . . . and the premise, shared by Jews in the West for perhaps two centuries, that Jewish interests and, indeed, survival were best served by an open, secular society promoting liberal values and tolerating a diversity of religious groups." Other writers have seen the Jews' liberalism as a response to anti-Semitism, which still haunts the United States and other nations. As long as Jews fear an upsurge of intolerance against them, as long as pockets of discrimination still exist, Jews will probably continue to support the politicians whom they regard as the staunchest defenders of civil liberties.

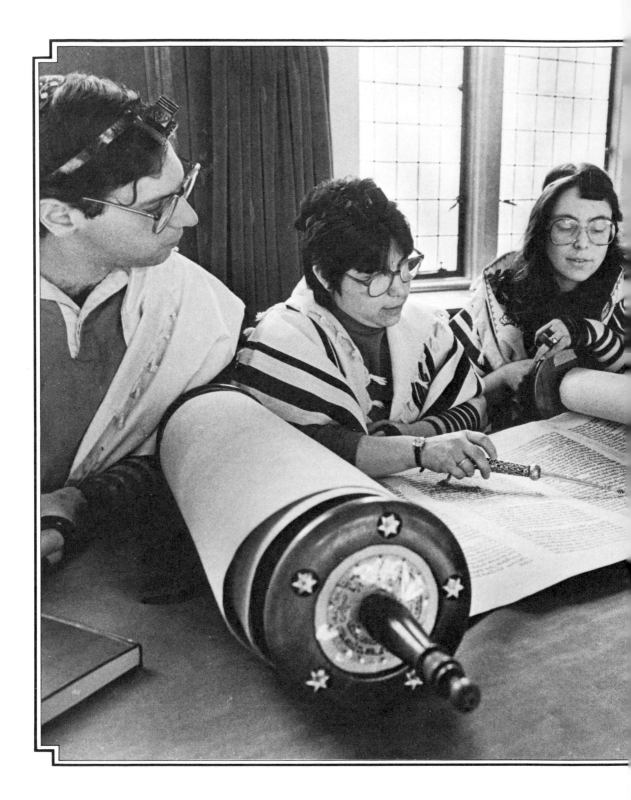

JEWISH AMERICANS TODAY

Jewish Americans in the 1990s are deeply concerned with several social and political issues that closely affect them. One of these issues is the deterioration of the relationship between the Jewish-American and African-American communities, who were once united in their support for the civil rights movement. Nowhere has the rift between blacks and Jews been more visible than in New York City. In the late 1980s, Ed Koch, New York's Jewish-American mayor, was defeated in his bid for re-election by African-American candidate David Dinkins. Koch had been criticized by black voters for insensitivity to African-American people and issues.

In August 1991, Dinkins received criticism from Jewish Americans after a tragic outbreak of racial violence in the Crown Heights neighborhood of Brooklyn. A car driven by a 27-year-old Hasidic Jew struck and killed a 7-year-old African-American boy, igniting four days of rioting in which crowds of blacks, mostly young men, harassed the area's Jewish residents; during the violence, a 29-year-old Jewish man was stabbed to death. Some Jews accused Dinkins of not taking the proper action to control the racial violence. Dinkins lost his re-election bid to Republican Rudolph Giuliani, who was strongly supported by New York's Orthodox Jewish population. New York's Jews were appalled by a second outbreak of violent anti-Semitism in 1994, when a gunman fired into a group of Orthodox students on the Brooklyn Bridge, killing two. One positive result of these incidents, however, was an increase in communication and unity among Jews from widely differing religious and social backgrounds.

Jewish Americans today are dismayed by the outspoken anti-Semitism of some fringe members of the Afri-

Mayor David Dinkins and Brooklyn Borough president Howard Golden speak to a crowd in riot-torn Crown Heights in 1991.

PEOPLE AGAINST HATE

FARRAKHANISM = ANTI-SEMITISM

SAY NO TO BIGOTRY

SHAME ON THE NAACP FOR EMBRACING A RACIST!

Jewish protestors express outrage at anti-Semitic comments made by Louis Farrakhan and other leaders in the black community.

can-American community, such as Louis Farrakhan and Khalid Abdul Muhammad of the Nation of Islam, a black Muslim organization. Farrakhan and Muhammad have gained attention with ludicrous and inaccurate accusations: for example, that Jews owned the majority of the slaves in the American South before the Civil War, or that there is a secret Jewish conspiracy to control the world. Although some mainstream black groups such as the Congressional Black Caucus have distanced themselves from the rantings of extremists like Farrakhan, other groups—including the NAACP, which numbered Jews among its founders—have been slow to repudiate anti-Semitism, further weakening the historic ties between American blacks and Jews.

Some of the antagonism felt by African Americans toward Jews today stems from the identification that some blacks feel with the Islamic faith. In the Middle East, the Jewish state of Israel has been involved for decades in a conflict with the Islamic states that surround it; by the 1990s, that conflict appeared to be headed toward resolution, as Israeli and Palestinian Arab leaders began a process of negotiation. The conflict—and the controversy over the peace process—have spilled over into American public life on several levels. As might be expected, American Jews take a close interest in Middle Eastern affairs and passionately support the Israeli state. There are, however, differences of opinion among Jews in the United States, just as there are in Israel, about whether or not Israel should permit the creation of a Palestinian Arab state on land that has been disputed between Israelis and Palestinian Arabs for several generations. Extremism on this issue has led to terrorism and violence by both Arabs and Jews, in the Middle East and in the United States: incidents include the 1993 bombing of the World Trade Center in New York City and 1994 attacks on five Jewish institutions in Chicago by Palestinians; the assassination in New York in 1990 of Meir Kahane, a militant rabbi who was opposed to the idea of a Palestinian Arab state; and the subsequent massacre of Palestinians in a Jerusalem mosque by an extremist follower of Kahane. Jews in the United States are fearful that the terrorism and violence that have plagued the peace process in the Middle East will be extended to America.

The Future of American Jews

Between 1880 and 1920 more than 3.5 million Jews arrived in the United States. Within a generation they had transformed their new homeland beyond reckoning, and they continue to do so. In areas as diverse as banking and filmmaking, Jews have made contributions that far outweigh their numbers. A century after the first great wave of refugees climbed out of steerage, Jewish Americans stand as an example for later immigrant groups who hope to attain equal success.

Of course, only a very small percentage of Jews in America have been millionaire bankers, film producers, labor activists, or Supreme Court justices. Most of them, like most members of every other ethnic group, have been ordinary people who have quietly gone about the business of working, making a home, and raising a family. Immigrants strove to become part of America by learning English, becoming citizens, and getting jobs. In the process, they moved away from some parts of their distinctive history. As Irving Howe wrote in *World of Our Fathers*:

> America exacted a price. Not that it "demanded" that the immigrant Jews repudiate their past, their religion, or their culture; nor that it "insisted" they give up the marks of their spiritual distinctiveness. American society, by its very nature, simply made it all but impossible for the culture of Yiddish to survive. It set for the east European Jews a trap or lure of the most pleasant kind. It allowed the Jews a life far more "normal" than anything their most visionary programs had foreseen, and all that it asked—it did not even ask, it merely rendered easy and persuasive—was that the Jews surrender their collective self.

Not all Jewish Americans would agree with this assessment; *surrender* is a strong word. But it is undeniable that acceptance and success in America have changed the relationship of modern Jews to each other and to their faith.

The children of the immigrants described by Howe became further assimilated into American society by attending public schools and colleges. They had opportunities to live and work in places that would have been inconceivable for their parents. Many of them made friends or even married outside the Jewish community. Third- and fourth-generation Jewish Americans are still further assimilated. Although few of them are rural, many of them live in the suburbs, and they are no longer as tightly concentrated in the northeastern metropolitan areas as their parents and grandparents were.

American Jews have also become increasingly secular. In a survey in the late 1980s, the majority of American Jews identified themselves as members of a cultural group rather than followers of a religion. Fewer than 20 percent of them attend weekly religious services; about 18 percent follow Jewish traditions regarding daily prayer, dietary laws, and observing the Sabbath. Roughly half of all Jewish Americans today will marry non-Jews.

In 1964, *Look* magazine predicted, "Young Jewish men and women are threatening the future of Judaism with their ever-increasing tendency to marry and raise their children outside the faith." Today, although intermarriage is more common than ever before, there has been an upsurge of religious commitment among some Jewish-American young people, and attendance at Hebrew schools and Jewish day schools is climbing in some communities for the first time in years, as is attendance at some synagogues. The question of continuity and identity occupies the attention of many Jews today, from parents in mixed marriages who wonder whether their children should be raised in the Jewish faith to scholars who ponder the future of American Judaism. Yet Judaism is a faith founded on historical consciousness, and as long as Jewish Americans remember their past and their connection to embattled Jewish minorities around the world, the link between American Jews and their roots will be unbroken. ～

FURTHER READING

Birmingham, Stephen. *The Rest of Us: The Rise of America's Eastern European Jews*. Boston: Little, Brown, 1984.

Dawidowicz, Lucy S. *On Equal Terms: Jews in America, 1881–1981*. New York: Holt, Rinehart & Winston, 1982.

Glazer, Nathan. *American Judaism*. 2nd ed. Chicago: University of Chicago Press, 1972.

Handlin, Oscar. *Adventures in Freedom: Three Hundred Years of Jewish Life in America*. Fort Washington, NY: Kennikat Press, 1971. Originally published in 1954.

Hertzberg, Arthur. *The Jews in America: Four Centuries of an Uneasy Encounter*. New York: Simon & Schuster, 1989.

Howe, Irving. *World of Our Fathers*. New York: Simon & Schuster, 1976.

Karp, Abraham J. *Golden Door to America: The Jewish Immigrant Experience*. New York: Viking, 1976.

Moore, Deborah Dash. *To the Golden Cities: Pursuing the American Jewish Dream to Miami and L.A.* New York: Free Press, 1994.

Plesur, Milton. *Jewish Life in Twentieth-Century America: Challenge and Accommodation*. Chicago: Nelson-Hall, 1982.

Rischin, Moses. *The Jews of North America*. Detroit: Wayne State University Press, 1987.

Sacher, Howard M. *A History of the Jews in America*. New York: Knopf, 1992.

Sanders, Ronald. *Shores of Refuge: A Hundred Years of Jewish Emigration*. New York: Henry Holt, 1988.

INDEX

Adler, Stella, 82–83
Africa, 19, 24, 26, 49
Aleichem, Sholom, 80
Alexander II, czar of Russia, 41
Allen, Woody, 85, 92
Alliance Art School, 95
American Federation of Labor
    (AFL), 110
American Revolution, 38–39, 47,
    51
Anti-Semitism, 13, 14, 25, 26–27,
    29, 37, 39–41, 44–46, 49, 51,
    102, 115, 117–20
Ashkenazim, 27

Baltimore, Maryland, 43, 58
Bellow, Saul, 93–94
Bernstein, Leonard, 87
"Borscht Belt," 85
Boston, Massachusetts, 43, 58, 106
Brandeis, Louis D., 106–7, 110
Brazil, 37
Brice, Fanny, 83–84
Bryant, Lena (Lane), 54

Cahan, Abraham, 75, 80
Canaan, 19, 21, 23, 33
Canada, 16, 47–49
Carter, Jimmy, 108
Charleston, South Carolina, 38, 39,
    51
Chicago, Illinois, 58, 60, 74, 93,
    105, 110, 120
Cincinnati, Ohio, 56, 64, 74
Cleveland, Ohio, 58, 74
Clinton, Bill, 108, 115
Conservative Judaism, 17
Copland, Aaron, 87
Cossacks, 29

Diaspora, 13, 23–32
Dinkins, David, 117–18
Disraeli, Benjamin, 29
Dubinsky, David, 75, 110, 111–12
Dylan, Bob, 89

Egypt, 13, 19, 20, 34
Einstein, Albert, 45, 104
Ellis Island, 43–44, 80
England, 16, 26, 28, 29, 31, 46,
    47–48
Exodus, 20–22

Farrakhan, Louis, 119
Flexner, Abraham, 104
France, 16, 26, 29, 31, 33, 39, 47,
    109
Frankfurter, Felix, 102, 107
French Revolution, 28, 39

Galveston, Texas, 43
German Jews, 13, 40, 44, 45, 51,
    53–56, 57, 58, 62, 64, 76, 95,
    106, 112
Germany, 17, 25, 27, 28, 29, 31,
    39–40, 45, 52, 53, 109
Gershwin, George, 86–87
Gershwin, Ira, 86
Ginsberg, Allen, 95
Ginsburg, Ruth Bader, 107–8
Gompers, Samuel, 75, 110–11
Goodman, Benny, 88–89
Gould, Glenn, 88
Greenberg, Hank, 98–99
Guggenheims, 76–77

Hanukkah, 34, 35
Hasidim, 29, 117
Hebrew Immigrant Aid Society
    (HIAS), 44
Hebrews, 19–22
Hebrew Union College, 56, 64
Herzl, Theodor, 31
Hitler, 40, 45
Holland, 28, 29, 37
Holocaust, 31, 48, 82, 91
Howe, Irving, 105, 115, 121
Hungary, 49

India, 19
International Ladies Garment

Workers Union (ILGWU), 110, 111
Iran, 17, 47
Iraq, 17, 31
Israel, 16, 17, 19, 23, 32, 47, 51, 120
Italy, 26, 109

Jerusalem, Israel, 23, 25, 27, 120
Jesus Christ, 25, 34
Jewish Americans
  as artists, 95–98
  assimilation, degree of, 17, 52, 57–58, 75, 90, 121–22
  in business and finance, 13, 14, 51–56, 59, 76–77
  and civil rights movement, 89, 115, 117
  early days in United States, 13, 37–40, 51–52
  and education, 14–15, 101–3
  in Hollywood, 14, 89–92
  immigration to the United States, 13, 14, 30–31, 32, 39–47, 53–57
  and intermarriage, 17, 121–22
  and journalism, 73–75, 80
  as judges, 106–8
  and labor movement, 74–75, 108–12
  in music, 85–89
  philanthropy, 62, 76–77
  and politics, 112–15
  religious groupings, 17
  religious practices, 33–35, 62–64, 73, 122
  restrictions on immigration, 44–46, 57
  and socialism, 75, 105, 110, 112, 115
  in sports, 98–99
  in theatre, 81–83
  in vaudeville, 83–85
  as writers, 79–81, 93–95, 104–5
Jewish Colonization Association, 48
Jewish Federation of Labor, 110
Jewish Workers Educational

Society, 110
Jews
  definition of, 17, 19
  dietary laws, 17, 33–34, 64
  history, 13, 19–32
  religious holidays, 34–35, 73, 81
Jolson, Al, 89
Jordan, 31
Judea, 19, 23

Kahane, Meir, 120
Kazin, Alfred, 105
Kibbutzim, 51
King, Martin Luther, Jr., 115
Koch, Ed, 117
Koufax, Sandy, 99

Landmanshaft, 61–63
Lauder, Estée, 54
League of Nations, 31
Lebanon, 31
Los Angeles, California, 16
Louisville, Kentucky, 104, 106

Mailer, Norman, 94
Malamud, Bernard, 94, 102
Memphis, Tennessee, 74
Mesopotamia, 25
Miami, Florida, 16
Morocco, 17, 19, 49
Moses, 20–22
Moskowitz, Belle, 113

Nazis, 27, 31, 46, 91, 114
Nevelson, Louise, 95, 97
Newport, Rhode Island, 39, 51
New York City, 16, 37, 39, 43, 44, 45, 51, 54, 57, 58, 62, 74, 76, 77, 79, 80, 82, 85, 88, 89, 92, 95, 97, 98, 102, 109, 110, 111, 117–18, 120

Orthodox Judaism, 17, 19, 29, 57, 62–63, 73, 74, 117, 118
Ozick, Cynthia, 95

Pale of Settlement, 29, 30, 32, 40,

41

Palestine, 13, 19, 23, 25, 27,
  31–32, 46
Passover, 34, 35
Philadelphia, Pennsylvania, 39, 43,
  51, 58, 74, 110
Pogroms, 29–30, 41, 59
Poland, 14, 27, 29, 62, 80, 109
Purim, 81

Reform Judaism, 17, 57, 62, 63–64,
  73
Rickover, Hyman, 105–6
Rodgers, Richard, 87
Roman Empire, 23–24
Romania, 41, 62
Roosevelt, Franklin D., 46, 107,
  114
Roosevelt, Theodore, 112
Rosh Hashanah, 34–35, 73
Roth, Philip, 94
Rothko, Mark, 95, 98
Rothschilds, 28
Rubenstein, Helena, 54, 76
Rubinstein, Arthur, 88
Russia, 14, 17, 29–30, 40–41, 42,
  80, 97, 98, 105. *See also* Soviet
  Union

Sabin, Albert, 15, 104
St. Louis, Missouri, 58, 74
Salinger, J. D., 94–95
Salk, Jonas, 15, 102, 104
San Francisco, California, 54–56
Savannah, Georgia, 38, 39, 51
Schiff, Jacob, 76
Selznick, David O., 90
Sephardim, 27, 38
Shahn, Ben, 95, 96–97
Shapiro, Irving S., 15
Shtetls, 14, 29, 40, 61, 62, 63, 64,
  80
Singer, Isaac Bashevis, 80–81

Singer, Israel Joshua, 80
Solomon, Haym, 39
Soviet Union, 16, 47, 49, 89
Spain, 25, 26, 27
Spielberg, Steven, 91
Spitz, Mark, 99
Stieglitz, Alfred, 95
Straus, Oscar S., 113
Strauss, Levi, 54–56
Stuyvesant, Peter, 37–38
Sweatshops, 44, 58–59, 61, 79,
  109–10, 111
Switzerland, 31
Syria, 17, 31

Talmud, 14, 25
Thalberg, Irving G., 90
"Tin Pan Alley," 86
Torah, 22, 23, 25
Touro Synagogue, 39
Trilling, Lionel, 15, 105
Turkey, 27, 31

United Hebrew Charities of New
  York, 62
United Hebrew Trades, 110
United Nations, 31

Walkowitz, Abraham, 95
War of 1812, 47–48
Washington, George, 39
Weber, Max, 95
Wilson, Woodrow, 107
Wise, Isaac Mayer, 64
World War I, 31, 44, 48, 76
World War II, 27, 31, 33, 45–46,
  48, 91, 105, 114

Yiddish, 33, 40, 74, 75, 79–83, 90,
  93, 94
Yom Kippur, 35, 73

Zionism, 31–32, 75

HOWARD MUGGAMIN is a lecturer on 20th-century studies with a special interest in Jewish-American culture. A frequent contributor to scholarly journals and other publications, he divides his time between New York City, Los Angeles, and Akron, Ohio.

SANDRA STOTSKY is director of the Institute on Writing, Reading, and Civic Education at the Harvard Graduate School of Education as well as a research associate there. She is also editor of *Research in the Teaching of English,* a journal sponsored by the National Council of Teachers of English.

Dr. Stotsky holds a bachelor of arts degree with distinction from the University of Michigan and a doctorate in education from the Harvard Graduate School of Education. She has taught on the elementary and high school levels and at Northeastern University, Curry College, and Harvard. Her work in education has ranged from serving on academic advisory boards to developing elementary and secondary curricula as a consultant to the Polish Ministry of Education. She has written numerous scholarly articles, curricular materials, encyclopedia entries, and reviews and is the author or co-author of three books on education.

REBECCA STEFOFF is a writer and editor who has published more than 50 nonfiction books for young adults. Many of her books deal with geography, environmental issues, and exploration, including the three-volume set *Extraordinary Explorers*. She has worked with Ronald Takaki in adapting *Strangers from a Distant Shore* into a 15-volume Chelsea House series, the ASIAN AMERICAN EXPERIENCE. Stefoff studied English at the University of Pennsylvania, where she taught for three years. She lives in Portland, Oregon.

REED UEDA is associate professor of history at Tufts University. He graduated summa cum laude with a bachelor of arts degree from UCLA, received master of arts degrees from both the University of Chicago and Harvard University, and received a doctorate in history from Harvard.

Dr. Ueda was research editor of the *Harvard Encyclopedia of American Ethnic Groups* and has served on the board of editors for *American Quarterly, Harvard Educational Review, Journal of Interdisciplinary History,* and *University of Chicago School Review*. He is the author of several books on ethnic studies, including *Postwar Immigrant America: A Social History, Ethnic Groups in History Textbooks,* and *Immigration*.

DANIEL PATRICK MOYNIHAN is the senior United States senator from New York. He is also the only person in American history to serve in the cabinets or subcabinets of four successive presidents–Kennedy, Johnson, Nixon, and Ford. Formerly a professor of government at Harvard University, he has written and edited many books, including *Beyond the Melting Pot, Ethnicity: Theory and Experience* (both with Nathan Glazer), *Loyalties,* andj*Family and Nation.*

Picture credits